CAREERS IN
BIOMEDICAL ENGINEERING

CAREERS IN
BIOMEDICAL ENGINEERING

Edited by

MICHAEL LEVIN-EPSTEIN

ACADEMIC PRESS

An imprint of Elsevier

Academic Press is an imprint of Elsevier
125 London Wall, London EC2Y 5AS, United Kingdom
525 B Street, Suite 1650, San Diego, CA 92101, United States
50 Hampshire Street, 5th Floor, Cambridge, MA 02139, United States
The Boulevard, Langford Lane, Kidlington, Oxford OX5 1GB, United Kingdom

Library of Congress Cataloging-in-Publication Data
A catalog record for this book is available from the Library of Congress

British Library Cataloguing-in-Publication Data
A catalogue record for this book is available from the British Library

ISBN: 978-0-12-814816-7

For information on all Academic Press publications visit our website at
https://www.elsevier.com/books-and-journals

**Working together
to grow libraries in
developing countries**

www.elsevier.com • www.bookaid.org

Publisher: Mara Conner
Acquisition Editor: Mara Conner
Editorial Project Manager: Gabriela D. Capille
Production Project Manager: Surya Narayanan Jayachandran
Cover Designer: Christian J. Bilbow

Typeset by TNQ Technologies

CONTENTS

LIST OF CONTRIBUTORS

David Braeutigam
Brautigan Enterprises LLC, Arlington, TX, United States; Healthcare Management Consultant, Arlington, TX, United States

Jayme Coates
The Luxi Group, New Hartford, CT, United States

Angelique Dawkins
Baylor Scott & White Health, Dallas, Texas, United States

David Harrington[†]

George Maliakal
Parkland Healthcare, Dallas, TX, United States

Frank R. Painter
Biomedical Engineering Department, University of Connecticut, Storrs, CT, United States

Asaki Takafumi
University of Hartford, West Hartford, CT, United States

[†]Deceased.

INTRODUCTION

Michael Levin-Epstein

More people than ever before are choosing biomedical engineering as their career. This is hardly surprising given that biomedical engineering is one of the most dynamic scientific areas in the healthcare space, with new medical devices being developed, and approved by the FDA, seemingly every week. This has created a plethora of new jobs and opportunities in this burgeoning field.

What is surprising, however, is that, to our knowledge, there's no book that details those jobs and opportunities in biomedical engineering—until now. This book discusses most of the significant opportunities in biomedical engineering, including data administration, biomechanics, clinical engineering, and cybersecurity. The book also includes chapters on the history of biomedical engineering, freelance opportunities, resources, and appendices.

The field of biomedical engineering is changing so rapidly that it's virtually impossible to include every new career opportunity. In future editions of this book, for example, we anticipate including chapters on clinical informatics and e-health.

As a starter book, we think you'll find this resource incredibly informative and valuable even if you're just considering a career in biomedical engineering. The information contained in these pages were written by some of the most respected professionals in their field and reflect decades of experience in biomedical engineering.

CHAPTER ONE

Historical Timeline

David Harrington[a],[†]

The timeline below was prepared several years ago as a way to put clinical engineering and biomedical engineering in an historical context.

13.9	Billion years ago, the Big Bang, expanding Universe
4.54	Billion years ago, the Earth formed
3.5	Billion years ago, primordial "soup" produced primitive life
6	Million years ago, man walked "upright" on two feet
1.7	Million years ago, cave paintings done in Lascaux, France
3000 BC	Bronze was introduced in Syria, was produced by adding tin to copper
300 BC	Erasistratus and Herophalius started to perform autopsies
100 BC	Ts'ai Lun invented paper
600	The first, still remaining, hospital—the Hotel Dieu—was established in Paris
600s	The first record of a wheel chair found on a stone slate in China
840	Al-Khwarizni founded the Arabic system of numbers and arithmetic
900	Rhazes described the use of plaster of Paris splints
1050	First pure food requirement passed in present day Germany, covered the brewing of beer
1100s	The first medical schools were established in Europe
1100s	The Knights of St. John began ambulance service in Europe
1240	Bacon made known the formula for gunpowder
1266	Peregrinus discovered magnetic ore and labeled the ends north and south
1275	Ether discovered by Spanish chemist Raymundus Lullius
1300s	The Black Death, a form of bubonic plague killed more than 25% of the European population
1317	Armati introduced spectacles
1440	Gutenberg invented the printing press

[a] David Harrington was an amazing contributor to the field of clinical engineering for decades, including writing numerous columns for ACCE News.
[†] Deceased.

Careers in Biomedical Engineering
ISBN 978-0-12-814816-7
https://doi.org/10.1016/B978-0-12-814816-7.00001-7

1490	da Venci invented the elevator
1498	Bristle tooth brush invented in China
1503	The first hospital was established in the West—in Santo Domingo, Hispaniola (now the Dominican Republic)
1574	William Oughtred invented the slide rule, replaced in the mid 1960s by computers and pocket calculators
1578	Harvey describes blood circulation in the human body, note that some say 1615
1585	Fabricius described valves in veins
1590	Compound microscope introduced by Janssens
1612	Medical thermometer demonstrated by Sanctorius
1618	Gilbert distinguished between electricity and magnetism, also conductor and insulators
1639	New College changed its name to Harvard
1640	Talbor introduced quinine to control fevers
1642	Pascal invented the mechanical calculator for addition and subtraction
1643	Torricelli invented the barometer
1646	Massachusetts passed the Stubbron Child Law, which allowed parents to execute sons as long as they were 16 years or older, it was repealed in 1973
1660	The lighted microscope demonstrated by van Leeuwenhoek
1662	Boyles law, the volume of air is inversely proportional to the pressure applied
1684	Newton published the laws of motion and gravity
1714	Mill patented the typewriter
1721	Increase Mather experiments with inoculations to control small pox
1724	The Fahrenheit temperature scale was introduced
1729	Stephen Gray, in England, distinguished between conductors and insulators of electricity
1733	Hales measures direct blood pressure in a horse
1738	Bernoulli reported the relationship between flow and pressure in fluids
1742	Celsius introduced the temperature scale bearing his name
1745	Discovery of the electric condenser called the Leyden jar
1745	de Vucanson used punched paper tape to control the pattern on a loom
1750	First patent issued for glue in Britain
1751	The first hospital in the US—Pennsylvania Hospital—opened in Philadelphia
1751	Ben Franklin published "Experiments and Observations on Electricity"
1755	Modern concrete introduced in Britain
1761	Giovanni Morgagni published a work on pathology

1765	The first medical school was established in the United States, in Philadelphia
1765	Watt demonstrated the modern steam engine
1771	New York Hospital opened
1774	Joseph Priestly isolated oxygen from air
1785	Joseph Bramhe patented the pump handle for draft beer
1786	Luigi Galvani, in Italy, noted that when dissecting frog legs they twitched when touched by the metal scalpel
1790	Thomas Wedgwood invents a method of transferring images to paper
1793	Eli Whitney introduced the cotton gin and the concept of standardized parts
1796	The first HMO started as the Boston Dispensary, the cost was $10.00 per year per family.
1796	Jenner discovered the immunological principle now known as vaccination
1798	Davy discovered the analgesic effect of nitrous oxide
1800	Volta discovers the galvanic cell
1800	Bichat identified organs by their different types of tissue, founding histology
1804	Hanaoka Seishu devised anesthesia, using 7 herbs, based off of both Chinese and Western medicine and performed a partial mastectomy, the patient lived
1810	Stethoscope invented by a French physician by the name of Laennec
1812	New England Journal of Medicine started publication
1815	Mass General opened for patients
1816	French physician Rene Laennec invented the stethoscope, some say 1819
1816	Physic introduced sutures that were absorbed into the wound
1818	Farady discovered the analgesic effects of ether
1818	Oersted discovered a magnetic field around a wire carrying an electric current
1826	Samuel Morey received a patent for the internal combustion engine
1827	Ohm's law introduced
1828	Webster's "American Dictionary of the English Language" published
1830	Niepce and Danguerre invented photography
1830	Henry and Faraday independently discovered electromagnetic
1831	Faraday produced a continuous current by rotating a metal disk in a magnetic field.
1831	Samuel Colt received a patent on the Six Shooter pistol
1832	Gauss introduced units of measurement for magnetism
1832	Saxton developed the rotating coil, alternating current generator
1834	Friction matches were introduced by Daniel Chapin
1836	Samuel Colt received at patent on the 6 shot revolver

1836	The Massachusetts Lunatic Hospital opened in Worcester MA. First state-owned asylum in the United States. Note being rebuilt for over 400 million in 2012
1837	First practical electric motor patented by Thomas Davenport
1839	Goodyear discovered how to vulcanization of rubber
1840	Morse patented the telegraph
1840	Baltimore College of Dental Surgery founded
1841	The adjustable wrench was invented by Loring Coes
1842	The first use of ether (by American surgeon Crawford Long) as a partial anesthetic to mask pain during dental surgery
1842	The Doppler effect documented
1843	Wheatstone Bridge introduced
1843	Joule quantified the relationship between heat and mechanical work
1844	Nitrous oxide introduced for clinical use, was discovered in 1798
1844	Goodyear patented the vulcanization of rubber
1844	Carl Benz was born, patent on gas engine in 1886
1845	Ballot proved the Doppler effect of sound
1845	Dentist Horace Wells used nitrous oxide for a tooth extraction
1845	Hollow needle invented by Irish physician Francis Rynd
1845	Kirchhoff introduced the laws of electric circuits
1845	Pneumatic tire patented by Robert Thompson
1846	Ether used in abdominal surgery by Morton and Warren at MGH
1846	Howe patented the sewing machine
1847	Chloroform used by Simpson for surgery and OB
1847	The American Medical Association formed
1847	Ludwig used a kymograph to record a blood pressure
1847	Thomas Edison born
1848	Lord Kelvin proposed the absolute temperature scale
1848	Women's Hospital in Philadelphia awards first nursing diplomas
1849	First woman, Elizabeth Blackwell, received a medical degree in the United States
1849	Count Sergei Lvovich took the first artificial studio photograph
1850	Opthalmoscope introduced by Hermann Von Helmholtz
1851	Mechanical refrigeration patented
1853	The hypodermic syringe introduced by Pravaz and Wood
1854	Florence Nightingale and her small team of nurses brought nursing care into prominence during the Crimean War in Turkey
1856	Bernard introduced the use of curare to block neuromuscular signal
1856	Henry Bessemer patented steel making process
1856	Alexander Parkes patented synthetic plastic made from cotton and wood cellulose
1857	Louis Pasteur demonstrated that organisms could be killed by heat
1857	Toilet paper introduced
1857	Tooth brush using hog hair bristles patented in the United States
1858	Lord Kelvin introduced the moving vane galvanometer

1859	Darwin proposed the theory of evolution through natural selection
1859	Lenoir invented the internal combustion engine
1859	International Red Cross founded by Henry Dumet, a Swiss businessman
1861	Marcey and Chauveau performed a cardiac catherization on a horse
1861	James Clerk Maxwell takes the first color photograph
1866	First ambulance service started
1867	Locking forceps, to clamp blood vessels, were introduced by Spenser Wells
1867	Nobel developed dynamite
1867	Lister discovered that carbolic acid as an antiseptic
1869	Hyatt invented celluloid the first synthetic plastic
1870	The Fick method of determining cardiac output was introduced
1870	Lister showed that surgical infections can be caused by airborne organisms and those organisms can be killed with the use of carbolic acid
1872	Guillaume Benjamin Armand Duchenne de Boulogne, pioneering neurophysiologist, described the resuscitation of a drowned girl with electricity
1872	Patent issued for vaseline
1872	Noble and Cooley received a patent on a machine to make wooden toothpicks
1872	Crowell receives a patent for a machine that makes square bottom paper bags
1873	The first nursing school was established in the United States
1875	Caton recorded an EEG of a rabbit using the galvanometer developed by Kelvin
1875	Chloral hydrate introduced as an injectable anesthetic agent
1876	The sphygmomanometer was invented.
1875	The telephone was invented by Bell
1876	Adolphus Busch introduces bottled beer
1876	Bell patented the telephone
1877	Pasteur vaccinated sheep for anthrax
1877	Siemens egain made electromedical devices
1879	Edison invents the electric light
1880	von Anrep demonstrated the local anesthetic effects for cocaine
1880	d'Arsonval introduced the moving coil galvanometer
1880	Edison invented the filament electric light
1880	Ringer solutions demonstrated
1881	American Red Cross founded by Clara Barton
1881	The International Congress of Electricians standardized measurements
1882	The tuberculosis bacillus discovered by Robert Koch in Germany
1883	First electric lighting system using overhead wires was installed in Roselle, NJ

1885	Photographic film on rolls introduced by Eastman Dry Plate Co.
1886	Punch cards for tabulating data introduced by Hollerith
1886	Steam sterilization introduced by von Bergmann
1886	Patent issued on gas engine
1887	Nikola Tesla develops the electric motor and a single electrode X-ray tube
1887	Hertz discovered electromagnetic radiation
1887	Michelson and Morley measured the speed of light
1887	Contact lenses introduced
1888	Carbon brushes introduced for electric motors, by vanDepoele
1888	Wallace Abbott started making drugs in Chicago, became AbbVie in 2013
1888	George Eastman received a patent on roll-film box camera
1888	Eastman also got a trademark for Kodak
1888	Ball point pen invented by John J. Loud
1889	Eastman started the production of photographic film
1889	Professor John Mc William, of Aberdeen University, described ventricular fibrillation
1890	First electrocution of a convict at Auburn prison in NY, William Kemmler
1890	Halsted and Bloodworth introduced the use of rubber gloves for surgery
1892	General electric formed
1892	Toothpaste in a tube introduced
1893	Willem Einthoven introduced the term "electrocardiogram" at a meeting of the Dutch Medical Association
1894	Vicks Vapo-Rub introduced for sales in the United States
1895	X-rays discovered by Willem Roentgen
1895	Hershey's introduced the chocolate bar
1896	Harvard Apparatus started producing medical devices for physician training in the United States
1896	Marconi experimented with wireless transmissions
1896	Riva-Rocca, Hill, and Barnard independently developed the "cuff" for indirect measurement of blood pressures
1896	Premature infants kept in an incubator as part of the sideshow on Coney Island, NY, about 40% lived. Note incubators were not common in hospital nurseries until the 1950s
1897	Asprin became a common drug
1897	Sir Ronald Ross identified a parasite in the gut of a mosquito that was the source of malaria
1898	Patent issued for dental floss
1899	The first commercial production of aspirin
1899	The Ford Motor company organized
1899	Pervost and Battelli created and arrested V Fib in mammals using both AC and DC currents

1899	Karel Frederik Wenchebach published a paper on cardiac arthythmias titled "On the analysis of irregular pulses"
1901	Trans-Atlantic radio
1901	Blood typing developed
1901	Patent issued for windshield wiper to Mary Anderson of Alabama
1901	First Walgreens Pharmacy opened
1903	EKG demonstrated by Einthoven
1903	First powered flight by the Wright brothers
1903	Ford Motor Co. incorporated
1904	Fleming discovered the rectifying vacuum tube
1904	Harvey Hubbell patented the electrical plug and outlet
1904	Safety razor introduced
1905	Korotkoff described the use of sounds in determining blood pressure
1906	DeForest invented the triode vacuum tube
1908	Model T Ford introduced along with the production line assembly
1909	Bakelite the first synthetic plastic was patented
1909	First SOS sent by SS Arapahoe off the coast of North Carolina
1910	Montgomery Ward offered employees a health insurance plan
1910	Sickle cell anemia described
1910	Richard Cabot studied 1000 autopsies and found that 40% had the wrong cause of death
1910	Morgan established that chromosomes as the carriers of heredity
1910	Rayon became commercially available, produced by American Viscose
1912	DeForest and Longwood developed the first vacuum tube amplifier
1912	The first recorded death due to radiation poisoning, Clarance Daley who worked for Thomas Edison
1912	The OREO cookie introduced for sale in the United States
1911	Charles Kettering demonstrated the electric start for automobiles
1911	Louis Chevrolet and William Durant founded the Chevrolet Moto Car Co.
1911	Computing-Tabulating-Recording Co, later known as IBM was incorporated in New York
1913	First gas station, (Gulf) opened in Pittsburgh, PA
1913	A patent for the zipper was issued to Gideon Sunback from New Jersey
1914	DeForest and Armstrong developed continuous oscillators, working independently
1914	Electric stop lights installed in Cleveland Ohio
1914	Toshiba entered the medical instrumentation market
1915	Midmark Corp. opened for business
1915	First Radiology Residency program in the United States
1915	Dr. Welch and William Allyn marketed the opthmaloscope
1915	First transcontinental phone call made, 2 wires 4750 miles long, each, 2960 tons of copper to make the wire, $20.75 for the first 3 min, $6.75 per minute after but only one conversation at a time

1916	Polio epidemic in United States 6000 died, 27,000 paralyzed
1916	Heparin discovered by Mclean and Howell
1917	Nikola Tesla detailed the principles regarding the frequency and power levels for radio location detection units
1918	500,000 died in United States in the flu epidemic
1918	General Motors buys the Chevrolet Motor Car Company
1919	Oregon is the first state to impose a gas tax of $0.01 per gallon
1920	KDKA, Pittsburgh, goes on the air as the first radio station
1920	Band Aid introduced by Johnson and Johnson
1920	Dr Jacob Lowe introduced a system called Foot-O-Scope that used X-rays to check on the fit of shoes. Banned in 1970 because of radiation levels
1921	Insulin isolated by Charles Best at the University of Toronto
1922	Hubert Mann, of the Cardiograph laboratory at Mount Sinai Hospital, described the vectorcardiogram.
1922	The US Army open a central repair depot for medical devices in St Louis
1922	Banting discovered insulin
1923	The first successful cardiac valve surgery, Brigham Hospital in Boston
1923	GE Healthcare established
1923	Patent issued on cotton swab
1924	Kleenex introduced
1924	IBM founded
1925	Colposcope invented by Hinselmann in Germany
1926	The concept of homeostasis in published by Walter Cannon
1926	DeForest developed a method of recording sound onto a the film of a motion picture
1927	Sanborn Instruments of Cambridge MA introduced the "portable" ECG recorder
1927	The infant formula Simulac developed at the Boston Floating Hospital for Children
1927	Bloodless surgery introduced by Dr. Cushing and W. T. Bovie at Huntington Hospital in Boston, commonly called electrosurgery. Some say 1926
1927	First television transmission in the United States
1928	Iron lung developed in Boston by Philip Drinker and Louis Shaw
1928	Penicillin discovered by Alexander Fleming
1928	Harold Edgerton develops the strobe light
1928	Farnsworth demonstrated the all electric television system
1929	Berger recorded the first human EEG signals
1929	First Blue Cross plan offered for municipal employees in Dallas Texas
1929	Bell Labs demonstrated the color television
1929	The Iron Lung for treatment of polio victims installed at Bellevue Hospital, designed by Drinker and Shaw

1930	Scotch tape introduced
1930	Twinkees introduced
1931	Baxter started producing IV solutions
1931	Patent issued on Tampons
1931	Dr. Albert Hyman patented the first "artificial cardiac pacemaker," which stimulates the heart by using a transthoracic needle
1933	Cyclopropane introduced
1933	Harry Jennings and his disabled friend Herbert Everest, both mechanical engineers, invented the lightweight steel collapsible wheelchair
1933	Philips introduced its first X-ray system
1933	Beer became legal in the United States
1934	Ruska invented the electron microscope
1935	Grass Instruments founded EEG
1935	Nylon invented by Wallace Carothers at DuPont, (also dated in 1934)
1935	Louis Minsk developed a photograph resist polymer at Kodak, which was used in semiconductors in the 1950s
1935	Beer sold in metal cans for the first time in the United States
1937	John Atanasoff at Iowa State University devised the digital computer
1937	Golden Gate Bridge opened for traffic on May 28
1937	First hospital blood bank opened at Cook County Hospital in Chicago, IL
1937	Patent for Nylon issued
1938	Passage of the Food, Drug and Cosmetic Act initiated the requirement that all drugs be approved by the FDA prior to being marketed in the United States
1938	Rh factor in blood discovered by Levine and Stetson
1938	Nylon bristle tooth brush introduced in the United States
1938	Roy Plunket discovered Teflon at DuPont
1939	Pan-Am introduced scheduled flights between the United States and Europe
1939	Armstrong developed FM radio transmissions
1939	Muller developed DDT
1939	Electric tooth brush invented in Switzerland
1939	Hewlett–Packard formed in Palo Alto Ca
1940	Rh factor in blood discovered by Landsteiner
1940	Mechlorethamine became the first effective chemotherapy drug for cancer
1940	The US Navy developed Radio Detection And Ranging system
1940	McDonald's open its first outlet in San Bernrdino CA
1940	First hockey game televised, Rangers beat the Canadians 6-2
1942	First controlled nuclear reaction at the University of Chicago
1942	Duct tape introduced
1943	First biomedical repair training program open at Army repair depot, a 3 month program

1943	Dirks invented the magnetic drum memory
1944	Willem Kolff demonstrated and artificial kidney using sausage skins
1944	First catheterization of the heart chambers and lung, Brigham Hospital, Boston
1945	Microwave oven
1945	Grand Rapids Michigan became the first United States city to add fluoride to drinking water
1946	ENIAC computer introduced, had 18,000 vacuum tubes and used 130,000W of power, Electronic Numerical Integrator and Computer
1946	Dunlee X-ray tube company founded
1946	CDC founded in Georgia
1946	The US Atomic Energy Commission started
1946	RCA started to mass produce television sets
1946	New Brunswick Scientific makers of laboratory devices was founded
1946	Tektronix, makers of test equipment, was founded in Portland Oregon
1947	Hill–Burton Act passed supporting hospital construction in the United States
1947	First artificial kidney machine perfected, Brigham Hospital, Boston
1947	Douglas Ring and W. Rae Young, Bell Lab engineers, proposed hexagonal cells for mobile phone in vehicles
1947	Edwin Land showed the Polaroid camera, black and white picture in 60s
1947	Microwave oven invented by Percy Spencer while working at Raytheon, he left school in the fifth grade
1948	Brattain and Bardeen working under William Shockley at Bell Labs co-discovered the physical phenomenon that led to the development of the transistor
1948	First cable TV network
1948	Polaroid introduces the "instant" camera
1948	World Health Organization founded
1948	Dr. Carl Walter invented the nonbreakable blood pack plastic blood collection bottle
1949	Medtronic founded
1949	Shockley discovered the junction transistor
1949	Montana physician Norman Holter develops a 75 pound backpack to record the ECG of the wearer and to transmit the signal to a reviewing instruments
1950	Vidicon developed allowing for fluoroscopic images without a luminescence screen
1950	External cardiac pacing demonstrated by John Hopps at University of Manitoba
1950	First nuclear medicine application
1950	Electronics for Medicine formed

1950	Color television demonstrated
1950	Olympus introduced the first commercial gastrocamera
1951	UNIVAC 1 computer released
1951	Bar Codes introduced
1951	The Joint Commission on Accreditation of Hospitals —the predecessor to today's JCAHO—was established
1951	Customer-dialed long distance telephone service became available
1951	Superglue introduced
1951	First coast-to-coast live broadcast of a TV program, a speech by Harry Truman
1952	The Apgar score for newborns developed by Virginia Apgar
1952	Paul Zoll MD at the BI in Boston used needle electrodes to restart and pace the heart
1953	First "open heart" operation
1953	First kidney transplant, between twin brothers, was done at Peter Brent Brigham Hospital in Boston
1953	Electrodyne formed
1953	PET scanner demonstrated by Gordon Brownwell at MIT/MGH
1953	Microwave oven introduced
1954	The rotating anode X-ray tube introduced
1954	Watson and Crick received the Nobel Prize for their elucidation of the double helix structure of DNA
1954	The MASER was demonstrated by Gordon and Townes of Bell Labs, a precursor to the LASER
1954	Wolf introduced the pistol grip rotatable endoscope with a wide angle telescope
1954	The computer language FORTRAN introduced by IBM
1954	The first atomic submarine, the Nautilus, was launched
1954	First coast-to-coast color broadcast on NBC, the Rose Parade
1954	First transplant of a kidney between brothers at the Brigham in Boston
1955	Salk's oral vaccine for poliomyelitis became generally available
1955	Zoll demonstrated ventricular pacing with thoracic electrodes
1956	Zoll demonstrated defibrillation using AC
1956	Cournand, Richards, and Forssman shared a Nobel Prize for their contributions to the advancement of cardiac catheterization. It was German, Werner Forssman who had passed a urological catheter from a vein in his right arm into his right atrium when he was a surgical intern in 1929 to first demonstrate the feasibility of this technique
1956	Heart-lung bypass technology received a significant boost with the development of the membrane oxygenator, which allowed extracorporeal circulation of the blood for days or even weeks without toxicity or hemolysis
1956	Radioimmunoassay developed by Yalow and Berson

1956	Ampex introduced the video tape recorder
1956	Halothane introduced
1956	Baxter introduced the first commercially built artificial kidney
1956	Storz introduced the flash illumination for endoscopes
1956	Gaymar founded and started making temperature control and patient comfort items
1957	The Emerson "postop" volume ventilator was introduced using a pressure cooker on a hot plate for humidifying the air stream and "chorboy" scrubbing pads as bacterial filters
1957	Sputnick goes into orbit
1957	The fiber endoscope introduced by Hirschowitz
1957	First atomic power plant open in Shippingport PA. Shut down in 1982
1957	Sabin polio vaccine came into use
1957	First digital photo scan is created by Russell A. Kirsch
1957	Kenneth Olson started Digital Equipment making computers
1958	Physician-engineer Forrest Bird introduced his Universal Medical Respirator, a little green box known far and wide as "The Bird."
1958	Gamma camera invented by Hal Anger
1958	Greatbach introduced the implanted pacemaker
1958	NASA formally created on July 29, 1958
1958	The IC is introduced by Jack Kilby of Texas Instruments
1958	Wolf introduced moving picture endoscope
1958	DARPA was established as a DoD agency
1958	NASA awarded Spacelabs the contract to develop the system to wireless monitor the vital signs of the Gemini astronauts.
1958	Roger Bacon developed the process of making carbon fibers to reinforce other material
1958	The United States launched its first communications satellite
1959	Dr. Georges Mathe, in France, performed the first bone marrow transplant
1959	The first monitored CCU was installed at Bethany Hospital in Missouri with Electrodyne Equipment
1959	Xerox introduces the plain paper copier
1959	First bone marrow transplant by Dr. Georges Mathe in France
1959	GPS introduced
1960	The use of ultrasound to image internal organs became a commercial product
1960	Townes and Schawlow received at patent for the laser
1960	The first LASER was built by Maiman at Hughes Aircraft using a ruby
1960	The "pill" was approved by the FDA for sale
1960	The "Ball Valve" introduced for cardiac surgery
1960	The Medtronic implantable pacer sells for $375.00
1960	IBM introduced the 360 business computer

1960	Storz introduced the cold light system for endoscopes
1960	Teflon-coated cooking utensils introduced for sales
1960	The Stryker Circolectric bed introduced for patients with spine problems
1961	The nation's growing "Medical Technology Imperative" is given a boost by President John F. Kennedy's call for the United States to put a man on the moon before the end of the decade
1961	Yuri Gagarin orbits the earth
1961	PhysioControl formed by Dr. Edmark
1961	Zoll reported the successful use of an implanted pacemaker to treat A-V block
1961	The "Pill" is introduced for birth control
1961	The Healthcare Information and Management Systems Society was founded
1961	Cochlear implant developed but reject by the body after about 6 months; it took until 1984 to work out all the problems and get FDA approval
1962	Severed arm successfully reattached at Mass General
1962	LINC developed at MIT, 1 kb of memory, sold for $43,600.00 the start of the PC
1962	Nick Holonyak Jr. invented the first LED that emits visible light
1962	AT&T Telestar 1 capable of relaying TV and phone signals launched
1963	Sanborn was sold to Hewlett Packard
1963	The DC Defibrillator, developed by Dr. Lown became commercially available, marketed by American Optical.
1963	De Bakey used an artificial heart during surgery
1963	Touch tone dialing introduced
1963	Joseph Carl and Robert Licklider created the first ARPANET transmission
1963	Robert Bruce and colleagues described the multistage treadmill exercise test
1964	Creation of a federally funded (National Heart Institute) Artificial Heart program drew upon the strong technological capabilities of the nation's aerospace contractors. Controversy about the relative promise of artificial organs and transplanted organs continues long after this funding was cutoff in the 1980s
1964	Staewen and Tabatznik published "Electrical shock hazards in electrocardiography and other laboratory procedures"
1964	The CO_2 LASER was introduced
1964	Dr. Michael De Bakey performed the first coronary artery bypass operation
1964	Medicare became law covering the medical expenses of retired and disabled
1964	Computer program MUMPS developed
1964	IBM introduces the System 360

1964	Tape loops introduced to store ECG data for up to 60 s in an ICU setting
1964	The United States Surgeon General, Luther Terry, issued a report stating that smoking is hazardous to your health
1964	The Beatles appeared on the Ed Sullivan show
1964	Ford Motor Company introduced the Mustang
1964	Kivlar introduced by DuPont
1965	Poptarts introduced
1965	Digital Equipment introduced the PDP-8
1965	First spacewalk taken by a Russian
1966	The ATM introduced at a Bankers convention
1967	Christian Barnard performed the first human whole-heart transplant in Capetown, South Africa, patient lived for 18 days
1967	The "explosion proof" patient monitor for the operating room was introduced into general hospitals by Electronics for Medicine
1967	A new professional trade group, the Association for the Advancement of Medical Instrumentation was founded
1967	Teflon-coated surgical instruments introduced, 7 years after Teflon-coated cookware
1967	The pocket calculator introduced
1968	Dr. Denton Cooley implanted a short-lived, non-FDA-approved artificial heart
1968	The Puritan Bennett model MA-1 ventilator became commercially available.
1968	Swan-Ganz catheter introduced
1968	The nation's first investor-owned hospital was opened in Nashville by the Hospital Corporation of America
1968	Michael DeBakey developed the left ventricular bypass pump
1968	An IABP developed by Arthur Kantrowitz went into commercial use sold by AVCO, base on the work done by Dwight Harkin in 1958
1968	The computer mouse was introduced
1968	The first 911 emergency call system was introduced in Haleyville Alabama, some say Bangor Maine
1968	Norman Shumway conducted the first heat transplant in the United States at Stanford
1969	A four-university network of large computers, known as the ARPAnet was created by the Department of Defense. This would later expand and morph into the Internet
1969	Electrodyne introduced the "segmented trace" scope a precursor to solid trace displays
1969	First installation of the Meditech system at Cape Cod Hospital
1969	ECRI published Health Devices
1969	The "Pig Valve" introduced as a cardiac valve replacement
1969	Man walked on the moon, Neil Armstrong and Buss Aldrin, July 20

1969	The polypectomy snare introduced by Olympus that allowed for the nonsurgical removal of polyps found during colonoscopy
1969	The implantable cardiac defibrillator was pioneered at the Sinai Hospital in Baltimore by Mirowski, Mower, and Staewen but not implanted until 1980
1970	The first "Solid Trace" display scope introduced by Electrodyne, using capacitance delay techniques, previously all display scopes were "bouncing ball"
1970	The first Earth Day proclaimed
1970	Corning introduce low-loss glass fibers that were developed into fiber optic items
1971	Fetal monitors introduced into the general hospital market by Corometrics
1971	Intel introduced the first microprocessor
1971	Texas Instruments released the pocket calculator
1971	Ralph Nader published an article in the March issue of the Ladies Home Journal on deaths in hospitals caused by electrical leakage
1971	Floppy disks revolutionized computer disk storage for small systems
1971	Soft contact lenses introduced 85 years after the hard contacts
1972	"Solid Trace" display using shift register technology introduced by Electrodyne, which was bought by Becton Dickinson
1972	NFPA requires isolated power systems in hospitals
1972	Atari releases PONG the first video game
1972	In December Apollo 17 the last moon landing took place by Eugene Cernan and Harrison Schmitt
1972	The United States launched Pioneer 10, the first artificial object to leave the solar system
1972	Dr. Fyodorov, in Russia, discovered the fundamentals of Lasik eye surgery
1972	The pocket calculator HP-35 was introduced by Hewlett Packard
1972	CT imaging invented by Hounsfield and Cormack
1973	The Williams-Steiger Act created OSHA
1973	Motorola introduced the first cellular portable telephone invented by Martin Cooper and was called the DynaTAC 8000X
1973	NASA launched Skylab
1974	CT first installed for clinical use
1974	Ethrane introduced
1974	Kellogg Foundations provides grants to Clinical Engineering shared services organizations
1974	Spacelabs introduced the Alpha series of monitors
1974	Aoyagi and Kishi of Nihon Kohden developed pulse oximetery
1975	Altair 8800 personal computer introduced for $400.00, 256 bytes of memory
1975	Gates and Allen introduce a BASIC computer
1975	Jobs, Sculley, Wayne, and Wozniak launch the Apple PC

1975	Digital camera introduced by Kodak
1976	The FDA's Medical Device Amendments, (PL94-295), which extended the FDA's jurisdiction to medical devices and created the Good Manufacturing Practices regulations
1976	Apple I computer became available at $666.66, in April of 1976
1977	The first in vitro fertilization, which resulted in the birth of Louise Brown in 1978
1977	Cardiologists Gruentzig and Simpson gain experience with angioplasty balloons leading to the introduction of coronary vascular stents
1977	Commodore PET, Apple II, Radio Shack TRS-80 all debuted
1979	Philips introduced the compact disc player
1979	Three Mile Island nuclear accident
1980	Forane introduced
1980	MRI was first applied
1981	DRG is introduced
1981	Bio introduces the first pulse oximeter to commercial distribution
1981	IBM comes out with its PC 5150
1982	US Counseling Services introduced "maintenance insurance" as a lower cost alternative to manufacturer full service contracts. The cost is typically at least 20% less than a comparable manufacturer contract. Similar offerings by other insurance companies quickly follow. This concept will bring about significant changes in the medical equipment maintenance aftermarket
1982	Barney Clark lives for 4 months with an artificial heart
1982	Commercial e-mail debuts
1983	Cyclosporine the antirejection drug was introduced allowing for more transplants
1983	Dr. Sam Maslak, of Acuson Corporation, developed the 128-channel computed sonography. Transducer rotating head transducers were replaced by this "phased array" system
1983	Cellular phone introduced
1983	PET demonstrated by Dr. Henry Wagner
1983	Technicare sold to Johnson & Johnson
1983	Compaq introduced its version of the PC
1984	The NMR, now called the MRI, introduced by Dr. Damadian of Fonar
1984	Apple Computer releases the Macintosh computer
1984	2000 + people died when the chemical plant in Bhopal India exploded
1985	Laser angioplasty demonstrated
1985	Irex sold to Johnson & Johnson
1985	GE buys Technicare (nuke medicine scanners)
1985	Fujinon introduced the video endoscope
1985	Windows 1.0 released by MicroSoft
1985	The first Internet domain was registered, symbolus.com, a computer company in Massachusetts

1986	Chernobyl accident occurred killing 31 at the time plus countless others from the release of radioactive material
1986	William Schroeder died on August 6 after 620 days with an artificial heart
1986	Wolf introduced the CCD endoscope system
1986	The space shuttle, Challenger, exploded 73 s after liftoff
1987	Noninvasive, robotic, radiosurgery system, called Accuray, based of the work of John Adler at Stanford was introduced
1988	SRI International begins research funded by DARPA, to allow surgeons to operate remotely on soldiers wounded on the battlefield
1988	Intravascular ultrasound imaging catheters were considered as interesting rather that practical devices in article published in the Journal of Vascular Surgery
1989	The North American College of Clinical Engineering was formed became ACCE in 1991
1989	The Berlin Wall was torn down
1989	Apple's laptop computer introduced
1989	First of 24 GPS satellites placed into orbit
1990	Diassonics sold to GE
1990	Introduction of coated stents for coronary arteries
1990	Human Genome projected by James Watson at the NIH to map the nucleotides contained in a human
1990	Assist International begins medical projects around the world installing ICU and imaging equipment in developing countries
1990	Hubble telescope put into orbit, repaired 2 years later
1990	The Web became available to everyone
1991	AOL dial up service
1991	Institute for Healthcare Improvement is formed to assist in the improvement of health care around the world
1992	Desflurane introduced
1992	Texting became available on the Net
1993	National healthcare system fails to be enacted by the US Congress
1994	The "Chunnel" between England and France was officially open to traffic
1994	GE purchases Marquette, note that Marquette purchased most of the GE monitoring technology when GE got out of that business in 1980
1995	Servoflurane introduced
1995	Yahoo debuts as a search engine
1995	Amazon becomes the on line book store
1995	eBay comes on line
1995	Fujinon introduces the high resolutions CCD chip for endoscopes
1996	Cardnial bought Pyxix
1997	ATL ultrasound sold to Philips
1997	SBT formed to make IV solutions in developing parts of the world

1997	Dolly, a sheep, was cloned in Scotland
1997	The Toyota Prius goes on sale in Japan, enters the United States market in 2001
1998	Multi slice CT introduced
1998	Google filed for incorporation in California
1998	Goggle and Pay Pal are introduced
1998	The iMAC is introduced
1998	Viagra introduced to market
1998	HIPAA was passed by congress
1999	The Blackberry is introduced
1999	PET/CT introduced
1999	Institute of Medicine published "To Err is Human: Building a Safer Healthcare System"
2000	Y2K proved to be a false alarm
2000	Agilent and ADAC sold to Philips
2000	Acuson sold to Siemens
2000	Philips Medical System acquires Hewlett Packard Medical
2001	The Pill Camera is introduced to study the total digestive track
2002	B&K sold to Dornier
2003	GE buys Instrumentarium, (included were Spacelabs that had to be sold off, Datex/Ohmeda and other companies
2003	The human genome project completed, was started in 1993
2004	Cardnial Health buys Alaris
2004	The disposable Pill Camera is introduced
2004	Spirt and Opportunity rovers land on mars
2004	Facebook launched in Boston by students
2005	High-definition endo systems introduced
2005	The first face transplant was performed in France
2006	Philips bought Witt Biomedical
2006	Twitter introduced on March 21
2007	Cardnial bought Viasys
2007	Ones purchased Eastman Kodak creating CareStream
2007	Eppendorf AG purchases New Brunswick equipment for $106 million
2007	Twitter is introduced
2009	CareFusion is spun out of Cardnail
2010	Philips acquired Burton Medical Products
2010	Double-hand transplant performed at the Brigham in Boston
2010	Real-time MRI imaging demonstrated in Germany
2010	Apple iPad goes on sale
2012	Baxter buys the dialysis portion of Gambro AG
2013	Grass Instruments, the originator of the EEG, purchased by Natus from Astro-Med
2016	An article in BJM stated that 251,000 people died because of medical mistakes

CHAPTER TWO

Database Management

George Maliakal
Parkland Healthcare, Dallas, TX, United States

When discussing database management in biomedical engineering, the first question might be "What is a database"? The simple answer is that a database is a listing or grouping of data, usually assembled in a way that can be accessed quickly. However, especially in today's world, a database can be as simple as an address book containing a list of names and addresses to something as sophisticated as a comprehensive set or data bank of thousands of customer records.

In the very beginnings of bookkeeping, something hand written in ledgers could have possibly been viewed as a form of a database. After all, it had columns with names and next to it information on each of the names and/or items identified by the name. This form of paper database eventually turned into computerized systems as computers became prevalent. One such database is a well-known product called Microsoft Access.

In the biomedical equipment world, seasoned professionals talk about how the simplest form of databases that was originally used was filing data on each asset in a file folder in a cabinet. Each folder was for an asset number and the folder contained all the paperwork related to that asset. It was either organized in the filing cabinet using a numbering sequence or by alphabetical order. This form of filing serves its purpose at the time, but eventually, it become cumbersome as the number of assets grew. In larger size hospitals today, the number of medical equipment assets can be in the many thousands and trying to manage the data by going through file folders may necessitate employing several full-time employees.

As the file folders and cabinets grew and as computers got more popular, moving these files into what is called a computerized, maintenance management system got off the ground. At the onset, it seemed the data were inputted into programs as simple as an Excel spreadsheet but eventually started being entered into databases like Microsoft Access. Soon, there were companies that stared focusing on building these databases specifically with medical equipment in mind.

Careers in Biomedical Engineering
ISBN 978-0-12-814816-7
https://doi.org/10.1016/B978-0-12-814816-7.00002-9
19

RELATIONAL DATABASES

Relational databases developed and that helped to push computerized, maintenance management systems ahead in the biomedical world. With relational databases, the data are stored in different tables with each table relating to another using some common identifier. For medical equipment tracking, there are many companies that sell their form of relational databases to biomedical engineering departments in hospitals so that medical equipment can be tracked. Each aspect of the medical equipment is then stored in tables with relationships built between tables that then are used to tie the information together and then accessed.

In using relational databases, accessing this data is made easier using what is known as a structured query language (SQL). It is a computer language whose only purpose seems to be to provide a way to query and manipulate data in the various tables that reside in a relational database. In this field, people have established careers by managing just this component of the database where they write code to manipulate and access the data within relational databases. This language can get very complicated and powerful especially when your database is huge using multiple tables. Using this language, you can create tables, move data, delete data, pull out data in specific patterns, and do many more tasks.

As the need for databases grows in the medical equipment world, more companies are marketing their versions of relational databases to biomedical departments within hospitals, and these companies have now started to create a drag-and-drop–type user interface to make it easier for users to deal with some of these deep SQL functions. This makes it easier for a biomedical staff member with little or no knowledge of SQL to manipulate data in a relational database by just moving graphical items on a screen. These can be as simple as block diagrams that point to other block diagrams with names of tables in the blocks that mean something to the biomed staff member. If there is a biomed staff member who knows some SQL, then they also provide an interface where they can use SQL commands directly to manipulate the database as needed.

Now, these companies are starting to host databases for the customers. This hosting function is, in addition to, the database being hosted by the hospital in the hospitals data center using the in-house information systems. These companies are not only doing simple databases but also are providing more sophisticated ways of extracting the data out of these databases in graphical forms or in basic reports. It seems possible that these companies can perform all these functions for hospital biomedical staff. These functions can be billed through a monthly or yearly fee. The details of the reports will be examined in discussions of the components of the computerized, maintenance, management systems.

ASSET RECORD NUMBER

In the biomedical world, each piece of medical equipment needs a way for it to be tracked in the hospital or facility that it resides in. Usually, it will involve the establishment of a serial number or a unique device identifier. Most hospitals or facilities use some type of numbering system that would denote an asset number, asset identifier, or biomed number. This is the number that uniquely identifies the medical device. This number is placed on the asset in a place where it can easily be identified by any and all hospital personal.

In tying this asset number to the computerized, maintenance management system, it becomes the identification used to house everything pertaining to the asset record in question. Additionally, this number is what a clinical staff would look at to place a trouble ticket into the Biomedical Engineering Department when they are having an issue with the medical device. The asset number is the main identifier that is placed into the computerized, maintenance management system by the biomedical engineering staff members to start the search for an asset in question. This is usually the starting point for the search of an asset in the computerized, maintenance management system.

When referencing certain medical equipment, the typical question you hear the biomedical engineering staff ask is "What is the asset number?" If a hospital has a call center that takes trouble tickets, they usually have access into the computerized, maintenance management system to enter the ticket, and the first question they will ask the person calling in the trouble ticket will be the same, "May I have the asset number of the device?"

After the call center staff enters the asset number, typically, their screen into the computerized, maintenance management system will give them a lot of the other details they need on the asset, and they can then continue to enter the problem statement from the clinical staff calling in. We will dive into the details of this flow later. Let us now look at a majority of common fields that is entered into the computerized, maintenance management system for each asset record along with some work flows as alluded to above that is run straight out of the computerized, maintenance management system.

Today, another functionality that is built into the asset number that the computerized, maintenance management system takes advantage of is what is called passive and active asset tags. These are tags that talk to the wireless system and report back its location to the computerized, maintenance management system. This way the biomed staff member can find the device easily in a hospital that is very large. This type of tagging and the infrastructure it takes to connect it to the computerized, maintenance management system does not come cheap.

The passive tag does not actively send out the location to the wireless network. It will most likely have to be scanned when it passes a point in the hall where the passive tag reader may be and that last seen location is reported to the computerized, maintenance management system via the wireless or wired network from the reader. For the active tag, the tag is in communication with the wireless network at a specified interval. This way it is actively sending location data to the computerized, maintenance management system.

With this type of a system tied to the computerized, maintenance management system, the database helps you find the device at your hospital and not just store data. In most cases, these tags do have an identification number that can be used as the asset number for the device as well. Keep in mind that the actual tags come at a hefty cost as well. The passive tags are cheaper, and the active tags are more expensive. In most cases, the active tags will have a maintenance cost as well due to it having a battery that you will have to replace at some interval. The battery is what provides it constant power to tell the wireless network where it is located at that instant in time.

MODEL NUMBER

The model number is another field that is tracked in the computerized, maintenance management system. This is a number specific to each manufacturer. Each manufacturer will have many different model numbers. This number is yet another way of identifying the device. When ordering parts this number is good in helping you to narrow down the parts for your specific device. Manufacturers also use this number to get information out to the community on product corrections or recalls. Within a computerized, maintenance management system, this number is typically one of the first few things you can see when looking up an asset record. In a relational database, the model number will be on a table so if you needed to query on the model number field the database will be able to give you all like models in a listing.

SERIAL NUMBER

The serial number is another method of tracking and asset. This is also stored in the computerized, maintenance management system. After a manufacturer gives a product a model number, the serial number further distinguishes the item with a more specific and unique identifier. In many cases, the serial number has identification systems embedded in it that the manufacturer uses to determine when the particular item was made. They can use this number to quickly identify different characteristics of the asset. When the biomed staff member is doing a repair on a piece of equipment and they look up the asset up in the computerized, maintenance management system, and then contact the manufacturer for parts, they can use the serial number to tell the biomed staff member if the item is still under warranty and what specific parts are available for that item.

Another reason it is important to have the serial number stored in the computerized, maintenance management system is for tracking the asset for things like recalls from the manufacturer. Typically recalls from the manufacturer is specified using a model number and then a range of serial numbers. The range might reflect a time when a group of assets was manufactured. Perhaps, there was a part or an item that was slightly below par and has become a weak point and has caused a failure, which then the manufacturer must recall and repair. So the manufacturer uses a range of serial numbers to let the customers know which items they must sequester or pull out and get the recall completed.

Often, the Food and Drug Administration (FDA) might request information from the biomed staff on recalls that we are done using a specified serial number range as well. It makes it easier for this information to be taken out of the computerized, maintenance management system if the serial number is stored in there. So as you can see it is very important to make sure that the serial number is stored and easily accessible from the computerized, maintenance management system.

MANUFACTURER NAME

The manufacturer name is another important piece of information that a biomed staff must or in the computerized, maintenance management system. This is the main avenue for the technician to determine who to contact for more specific needs for the asset record. For example, when the biomed staff is perhaps doing a repair on a piece of equipment, and they must call the manufacturer for specifics on parts and or help on the repair, it would be prudent to be able to look in the computerized, maintenance management system and be able to immediately determine who the manufacturer is. Along with the manufacturer other important aspect to store would be the contact information related to the manufacturer.

When storing the manufacturer name in the computerized, maintenance management system, it would be important to store some additional information about the manufacturer on different tables as well. One such example would be the contact phone number for the manufacturer. As a biomedical staff member you would want to be able to quickly access the phone number so that you can call the manufacturer as needed. In a relational database, the phone number would be stored in another table that would be tied to the manufacturer using a common field.

Another field that the biomed staff member would need in the computerized, maintenance management system would be the address for the manufacturer. The address is needed quickly for many reasons such as being able to ship the asset back to the manufacturer for any number of reasons such as depot repair or for recall actions. Once again, the address would be stored in different tables within the relational database. This would be tied together using a common field among tables as other fields mentioned above.

In using a relational database, another field to have would be whether this manufacturer allows for third-party parts to be used on their assets. Typically, this can be denoted by specifying a small field that says that the manufacturer must be used for parts. The computerized, maintenance management system might typically present this in a Graphical User Interface (GUI) interface that allows you to put in a check mark. However, it is typically yet another table, and this is also a searchable field for the biomed staff member if needed. Using SQL would be the best method to search even such a field as a checkmark.

UNIQUE DEVICE IDENTIFIER

The unique identifier is a relatively newer field that will be tracked in most databases. This is a field that was required by the FDA to be just as the name suggests a unique identifier that identifies that specific asset. Most database manufacturers have this as a field available for you to fill in.

MAINTENANCE STRATEGY

Maintenance strategy is just as the name suggests the strategy that you use to maintain the medical equipment or asset. There are a few options for how a device is maintained, and this information has to be stored in the computerized, maintenance management system. The most common maintenance strategy is to do what the manufacturer recommends that you must do. This is commonly used for things that are considered to be life support and lasers within a hospital. Typically, non–life-support equipment and nonlaser pieces of equipment have the option of using an alternate maintenance strategy.

An "alternate" maintenance strategy is exactly as the name suggests an alternate strategy that is different from what the manufacturer recommends. If you choose to put a piece of medical equipment in an alternate maintenance strategy in the computerized, maintenance management system, there are some things you must do prior to doing that. You must have a record showing why it is that you are doing what you are doing and provide backup data for what you say. If you choose to decrease the maintenance requirement, then you must show the proof and reasoning behind why you decrease the maintenance requirements. Typically, this proof would be something that you should be able to access via the computerized, maintenance management system if at all possible.

CORRECTIVE MAINTENANCE (CM) WORK ORDERS AND FLOW

The computerized, maintenance management system is very important in tracking and creating corrective maintenance work orders for an asset record. This is a very important function that must be tracked and stored in the database for regulatory reasons within the hospital. All historical work orders must tell a story within the computerized, maintenance management system about the corrective maintenance that was done on an asset record since the time it came into the hospital system.

One way that a corrective maintenance work order can be created within the computerized, maintenance management system is for the biomed staff member to create the work order themselves within the system against a particular asset record. This can be done using a GUI interface that sits in front of the tables that are stored in the server. Typically, when the biomed staff member opens the application and enters the asset number in the work order creation section, the remaining pertinent fields should show up on the same page. These fields would be everything from serial number to manufacturer and model information and much more as defined by the biomed department.

Another workflow for how a corrective maintenance work order can be created within the computerized, maintenance management system is for the call center to enter the corrective call into the database. Typically, for this kind of an entry, the biomed department would set up a separate GUI interface accessible to the call center staff. One reason is that you do not want call center staff to be able to get pretty deep into the database and access data and or inadvertently change any data.

For this reason, a separate GUI interface can be set up through the computerized, maintenance management system so that when a call comes in the call center, the staff can create a corrective maintenance work order. It would be predetermined exactly what fields they would have access to view and what Fields they would be able to actually enter data into based on the call coming in.

The page that is set up for the call center staff can be created using the GUI interface that is available in the computerized, maintenance management system. It may be simple enough for the biomed staff member to create or maybe somebody who manages the database might be able to do it. The creation of this interface would require a little bit of SQL knowledge perhaps, or it may be simple as drag and drop using a GUI interface that allows you to build another page specific for the call center staff.

An additional workflow that can be set up within the computerized, maintenance management system for work order entry is to have yet another page set up for clinical staff to directly enter the work order into the database. Once again, setting up this page can be done using a GUI interface. The database manager or biomed staff member will need to create a page and put a link to it on the hospital's Intranet page so that the internal clinical staff members can get to that link. Once they click on the link, they will then be taken to a corrective maintenance request page, which actually resides within the computerized management system.

This page can be custom made to allow the clinical staff members to see exactly what they need to have in order to place a corrective maintenance work order. Typically, one of the first things you would want to have is the asset number field so that the clinical staff member can put that in. Once that is put in, the database will typically be able to grab all the other fields necessary like model number, serial number, and location and displayed on the screen. At this point, you will also need a field where the clinical person entering the corrective maintenance work order can type in exactly what the problem is that they are having with this particular piece of equipment. This field is typically free text.

Once the clinical person types in the problem the next step for them would be to submit the work order by selecting the save option most likely.

Because it is the hospital's Intranet, the assumption here is that the clinical person would have had to log into their computer and the system is using their hospital login information, and the same info is being pushed into the database when they logged into the work order entry page. What this allows the computerized, maintenance management system to do is grab the clinical persons login credentials and automatically put in the information as to who placed the call.

After the clinical staff enters the call into the computerized, maintenance management system, a workflow can be set up such that the call gets sent to the appropriate biomed person to acknowledge and do the work. This workflow is typically managed through a GUI interface within the database. Keep in mind that this can be done using SQL as well, but most database vendors will provide a GUI interface that allows you to set up the workflow using graphics on the screen to design a workflow.

A typical workflow might be that after the clinical person enters the call, it gets routed through the system to the biomed apartment based on if it is an imaging call or a biomed call. At that point, staff members within either department may have an option to acknowledge the work order using the database.

After acknowledging the work order, they would then have to contact the customer and take care of the problem. After the asset has been repaired, the biomed staff member would be required to fill in all the details of the repair within the work order itself. This information is going to be stored in the database so that other staff members can review it or to be pulled up later for review by a regulatory organization. Some additional items that the biomed staff member may be required to enter into the computerized, maintenance management system would be things like the amount of time that was used to do the repair work, as well as all of the parts that were used to do the repair work, and also the cost of the parts. Additionally, depending on the organization that you are working for, the requirement may be there to enter in if a third party or vendor came in for doing the service. Typically, this would be for monitoring how the money is spent on the repair work, which in turn justifies having a biomed staff member on site working on the device. And finally one additional component that you may have to record is if the device has contract work done on it as well.

PARTS ENTRY

Managing parts inside of the computerized, maintenance management system is a challenge all by itself. These days any computerized, maintenance management system that you purchase from any vendor out there will give you the option to add in parts. The biomed staff will have the option to generate multiple stockrooms within the database. Each stockroom can be for any specific grouping of parts, for example, you may want to have a stockroom specifically for imaging parts or you may want a stockroom specifically for a particular modality like infant warmers. Whichever the way you do it within each stockroom, you can have multiple parts. For each part you can put in the quantity that you currently have inside the stockroom.

One other key feature is that the database can be set up to notify you when the part goes below a set par level. This is very important so that you will never run out of parts. Because one of the worst things to have happen is if you are in the middle of the repair and go look for a part and you realize that the last one has already been taken, and no one has replenished the item. Would this kind of a par level reminder that may come out in the form of an e-mail or an alert the biomed staff will then be able to go ahead and place an order for the part and make sure it is replenished. When that order comes in the available quantity, the stockroom must be increased to the amount that was ordered.

Another key feature inside of the parts table is the fact that you are able to put the price of the part in the system. This price will then calculate into the total cost of the repair work order. This will be a price that can change from time to time depending on part availability or as the manufacturer decides to increase or lower the price. When this happens, the biomed staff has the ability to change the price and make corrections.

Keep in mind that each stockroom and all the parts that you have in each of the stockrooms are on different tables possibly within the parts section. So inevitably one of the key features that this will allow you to have is the ability to report on parts and the various ways that you might want to see what has been done with these parts. This will be further investigated in the reporting section below.

VENDOR SERVICE

Services provided by the vendor are also something that is documented in the computerized, maintenance management system. The main reason for this is to later on pull out reports that will help you figure out where the money is going. Typically, the way this is done is by creating a section in the time charges that includes specifically vendor services. This once again goes on a separate table and is related to the time charge table typically.

Some of the items that are usually documented within the vendor services section is the amount of time that the vendor took to perform the work. The other component is usually the cost that was specific to the vendor service that was provided. Once again this is where the cost is able to be pulled out later that were specific for vendor services. And once again parts that are very specific to what the vendor did will be entered here as well. This will have a cost associated with it as well so that those specific parts can be tracked separately if needed.

Within an in-house biomed shop, outside vendor use would be rare, but at the same time, there will be some specialties that would require the vendor be called out. Financially, it would be very prudent to track these independently in the database because when the leadership of the hospital is looking for details and how money is being spent, this is where you can readily take the data out and display it as needed. Once again, it is another way that the computerized, maintenance management system can provide data and make it easy to track cost.

SERVICE CONTRACTS

Service contracts are another way to provide service to perform maintenance and or corrective work on a piece of medical equipment. As the name states, this is a contract between the hospital and the manufacturer or vendor providing the service. Typically details are written out in the contract of what the expectation is from the hospital as well as what the expectation is from the vendor. This is something that is reviewed by the Contracting Department within the hospital as well as the biomed department in the hospital to ensure that the necessary service is performed. Before the contract is signed the lawyers within the hospital will also review and make any changes as needed from a legal perspective. Usually, the contract is going to be for multiyear depending on how long the medical equipment is expected to be in the facility. There is always a cost–benefit for doing multiyear contracts.

Most often, the biomed department will have to justify having to get a contract as opposed to doing work using the in-house biomed staff. This is mainly accomplished by doing some investigations within the computerized, maintenance management system unless the medical equipment has no other option other than for the manufacturer to provide service. There are lots of companies out there that have very specific things that they must do themselves and cannot have a nonqualified person work on the equipment. In these cases, there is really no other way but to have a contract on file.

The principal reason that the computerized, maintenance management system is used here is to first justify the contract by reviewing the history within the database on the equipment in question. If database demonstrates the cost–benefit whether it is for parts or service, then this would be good enough justification to go ahead and put the device on a contract. Once the contract is in place, the computerized, maintenance management system will have a section where you can actually enter the contract into the database.

Once the contract is entered in the computerized, maintenance management system, there are some options to make life easier for the biomed staff member. All of the assets that are tied to this contract can be pointed at this contract within the system itself. The benefit of doing this is that when any type of work order gets opened against these assets in question, the database will immediately tell you that there is an active service contract on this device. What this allows you to do is to start the process immediately to get the work order addressed by the manufacturer providing the service contract. The biomed staff will typically get an option to call out the manufacturer by displaying the manufacturer information that is on the contract.

After the services are done, the vendor or manufacturer will typically give the biomed staff a piece of paper that list out what was done and the cost of the items that were used and the labor for the technician that came out. Once the biomed staff receives this, it would be prudent to take these data and enter it into the asset record history within the work order. Usually, one would want to split out the labor and parts cost, even though it is on contract and store it in the database. Reason for this is to later be able to pull this out and say this is what we spend on this device on contract versus this is what it would have cost if we did not have contract. So what the computerized, maintenance management system is allowing you to do is to justify the contracts that you have by using it this way. By doing this, to state the obvious the biomed department may also find that a contract is not needed possibly if not enough services were needed through the contract.

PREVENTIVE MAINTENANCE TASK AND SCHEDULES

Another important function of the computerized, maintenance management system is to keep track of preventive maintenance tasks and schedules. This is a very important function in the biomed environment because there are a lot of regulatory items connected to this. All preventive maintenance must be tracked within the database, and it must be tracked for historical purposes.

When an asset is initially entered into the computerized, maintenance management system, the biomed staff member must ensure that it requires some sort of maintenance or it can be left as-is. As mentioned above, one of the ways to go about doing this is to verify what the manufacturer requires and do that accordingly to their steps. If it requires a periodic maintenance, then the next step would be to create within the computerized, maintenance management system a schedule for this particular asset.

The schedule within the system can be created in whatever time that is necessary as in it can be annual semiannual monthly or quarterly. What this enables the system to do is once you select how periodic you need the schedule to be the computerized, maintenance management system, it will create a preventive maintenance work order automatically according to that periodic schedule. You can even tell the system that you want the schedule to begin at the first of the month or you can even have it open up on the exact date in the month from when you close the preventive maintenance work order the last time.

Another component of preventive maintenance is that the biomed staff member can also put in the specific tasks that are involved in getting this maintenance done. If this is done you must ensure that the detail specified by the manufacturer is followed. These tasks can also be put into a form of question answer system where the database prompts the biomed staff member for answers to each of the steps within the list of tasks. As the prompts come on the screen, the staff member can enter the answers and each answer will be stored in the database for historical records attached to this particular work order.

REPORTING

One of the most powerful components of the computerized, maintenance management system is the ability for it to create reports specific to what anyone would need in the organization. Some of the reports can be done for productivity of the biomed staff. One such example is time reports on these biomed staff members. These reports can be made available to each individual as well as the team or can be kept by the management staff to monitor how much time is being entered by the biomed staff. The importance of having this information is that you are adding what it is that was done to the asset record within the history, and it includes the amount of time the staff member put in on that work. Typically, the biomed department will want to know how much time the staff is spending on repairs and maintenance to show productivity to upper management, and this would be a perfect way to pull that kind of a report out using the database.

Another kind of reporting that is useful from the database is to see how many work orders are being done and of what type. This would be important to find trends within the organization. These trends can be then used to educate clinical staff as needed. For example, if you are noticing in the database that there are lots of calls being put in for battery charge issues on a particular asset, you may be able to look yet the reasons for this within the database, and it could be that the staff is failing to plug in the device when it is not in use. A simple trend needed, as this can be found by looking in the database and then educating the clinical staff. So you can see how the computerized, maintenance management system can actually help prevent failures by looking at reports on trends.

Another report that you might be able to pull out from the computerized, maintenance management system can be a report on parts and the prices for all the parts that are being used. There is a lot of power in these data because it can be used to determine if there are more cost–effective ways to purchase parts. The department may look at going to third-party sources for parts to get it cheaper. Or the department may even look at adding a parts contract from the manufacturer or even a full contract from the manufacturer depending on what the costs are. These reports can also what you see how many parts are being used of a certain type. This might even help you determine how much to keep on hand so that you can anticipate and reduce the downtime on medical equipment.

Finance may require a report from the computerized, maintenance management system to determine how much the department is costing. So this might include a report for finance that has everything from what the staff does to parts and labor all the way to contracts and how much is being spent on contracts. These kind of data are often very powerful for the accounting group so that they can help justify having a biomedical engineering group within the hospital system itself as opposed to outsourcing the entire group. So this type of a report can be used by the biomed managers also to fine-tune the program so that the department is a value to the organization. So as you can see, the reporting function alone create such a deep impact for the biomedical engineering department. It is not just a way of tracking medical equipment asset records.

MANAGING RECALLS

Another important function that the computerized, maintenance management system can provide the biomed staff is to help track and manage recalls. Recalls are very important aspect of the medical equipment world because a manufacturer may find a flaw or a defect that needs to be corrected. Not correcting it may lead to patient safety issue. This is such an important item that the FDA even tracks it to make sure that hospitals get recalls completed in a timely manner with the help of the manufacturer. The FDA may even review the hospital records specific to recalls.

One way of actually tracking recalls in the computerized, maintenance management system can be by creating a recall type work order against the asset record. Because the database provides options for creating many different types of work orders, this will distinguish at this particular one is a recall type. Once the work order is opened against the asset, the biomed staff will have the option of researching the recall to determine what needs to be done at their facility against this particular asset. The actual recall solution may involve bringing the vendor on-site to have them do a remediation on the device. If this is done, the biomed staff member must document within the work order the details of what was done and when it was done by the vendor. Yet another option might be that the biomed staff has the manufacturer send them the part that needs to be installed on the device for remediation. If this is the option that is chosen, the staff member must still document all of the details all the way to the point of completion. The main reason for this as stated above is that FDA has the option to verify that this was complete. To do this, the agency may ask for your records from within the database. If and when FDA asks for these records, the biomed staff will need to recover the history by running a report or pulling up the individual asset record and printing the details out for the FDA official.

MEDICAL EQUIPMENT PLANNING

One other aspect that the computerized, maintenance management system can be used for within the biomed department is to plan for medical equipment replacement. The database these days has many options for tracking different parameters of an asset to help you determine when the asset needs to be replaced. Some of these fields might be the purchase date, the cost of the device when it was purchased, the replacement cost which may be a marked-up price above the discount rate that the hospital gets, an autocalculated field that determines the cost of service to date, and perhaps, even a depreciation field that might be autocalculated. Additionally, there may be an option to enter user satisfaction to calculate that into the score as well.

The computerized, maintenance management system at this point can take all of the data above and assign a scoring matrix to it, which allows you to come up with a number that you can then use to determine if the item needs to be replaced or it has some more life left within the facility. So at this point, annually, a report can be run against this field that is calculated out using all of the above items and you will be able to forecast what needs to be replaced and when it needs to be replaced. This becomes a very powerful tool, as the biomed staff will be able to provide detailed information using metrics described above to finance to see where money needs to be spent. In addition, to providing information to finance, this is a good tool for clinical managers to get information from it so that they can make a decision on if they want to proceed with trying to replace something that they have in their department.

MANAGING CMMS

There are a few options on how to manage the computerized, maintenance management system within the hospital system. One option is to have the entire management of it be done by the database manufacturer. What this would mean is that the server would be hosted remotely at the manufacturer's location, and they would be keeping the data for the hospital. They would also help with maintenance and management of the server. The only thing the biomed staff would have to do is to make sure that their data get entered, and all of the management and reporting can be provided by the manufacturer for a reasonable price.

Another way to have the system managed is to have a dedicated person within the biomed department who takes care of the system. The system would still have to reside in the data center that belongs to the hospital, but the management can be done by the biomed staff member. This would mean some basic training, and knowledge of databases would be required. This would also mean that this person would be the one who does all of the management-related functions within the database and us can lead to a single point of failure if there is not someone to back up this person. There are hospitals that prefer to go this route and have had successes.

A final option for managing the computerized, maintenance management system would be to have the hospitals Information Systems professionals take care of it. This would perhaps mean that the system would be handled by a group that handles servers and databases within Information Systems. This would help ensure that there is not a single point of failure, but rather the team would handle the database management. This would also mean that there needs to be constant and consistent communication between biomed staff members and the information management team members as needed. There are a number of facilities that choose to do database management in this manner and have had successes as well.

As you can see, the computerized, maintenance management system has become a very powerful tool for the biomed staff. It is no longer just a place to store data. It has multiple functions, all of which can be used to bring a lot of power to the staff. One thing to always remember is that this is a place that will tell a story about the asset record. Every step it took since it entered the hospital facility. From initial acceptance, to the details of the asset, to all the preventive and corrective maintenance work that was done, all the parts that were used, all the labor that was put into the asset, all the recalls that were done, and finally the retirement and disposal of the asset.

CAREER OPTIONS

Career options are pretty vast for managing the computerized, maintenance management systems. As far as college goes, one can take any technology-based track, but it is important to try to get some training in basic databases. Also need to focus on SQL-related training as well because most of these databases are relational tables that need to be manipulated. There are lots of options available through universities to get specific SQL training as needed. There are also modules available through online training that a person can take.

Once in a career, within a hospital, there are some options for getting into this area. With the appropriate training a person can start within the IT department within the hospital. It is usually in the IT department where these databases are built. Here, depending on the facility and the location within country, the salary options are anywhere from $50k to $100k. This also depends on the experience as well. Typical job titles in this area can be anything from IT database manager to software systems manager.

Within a hospital, another option for being a database administrator would be as a clinical engineer working within the clinical engineering department itself. Within this role, the salary range is still about the same as above depending on the region of the country you are working in. One of the key differences from the roll above inside of IT is that this particular role will have more expertise in medical equipment as well.

Yet another area that one may obtain a job managing databases would be with the actual vendor itself. There are lots of vendors out there who need database administrators working on managing databases for their customers. The salary range remains about the same but you will be known as a database administrator for the most part. The skill sets required would still be the same as described above for the information systems person. The main difference here would be that one would be working directly for the manufacturer.

In comparing the various opportunities above, there is not anyone that is better than the other. It would ultimately come down to what a person is comfortable doing and where that person is comfortable working. And finally training as described above can be anything in a technical field but of course if the person has some detailed knowledge of the medical equipment world, this particular component of managing medical devices inventory will be a whole lot easier.

CHAPTER THREE

Biomedical Engineering

Jayme Coates[1], Asaki Takafumi[2]
[1]The Luxi Group, New Hartford, CT, United States; [2]University of Hartford, West Hartford, CT, United States

Biomedical engineering is the design, development, manufacturing, and maintenance of medical products and therapies. While this may sound straightforward, medical products can include everything from a Band-Aid to an implantable heart pump to an MRI machine to a tissue-engineered product.

Biomedical engineering is a discipline that combines engineering principles with biology. While not necessary, most biomedical engineers have a background in engineering; biomedical engineers combine an engineering background with anatomy, physiology, and biology in some way. This combination may be readily apparent, for example, when it comes to designing prosthesis or orthopedic implants, but it also can be much more abstract when it involves working on products incorporating genetics, cell, or tissue engineering. Being a biomedical engineer can require utilizing engineering techniques learned in schools, or it can combine the technical knowledge with soft skills such as sales, management, interpretation, teaching, or marketing. In a field with such enormous opportunities as biomedical engineering, a few key characteristics for success stand out inquisitive nature, analytical nature, ability to follow and understand regulations, and a passion for helping people.

HISTORY

Science and engineering disciplines were evolved and developed over many years as a result of endless curiosity and enhancements to the quality of human life. Evolution of medicine, dental science, biology, chemistry, or any biological life science, as well as medical technology, demands continuous innovation of engineering developments. In other words, engineering and technical advancements helped the life science explorations. Scientists and medical professions desire to see more details of organs or cells, which leads to develop more powerful instrumentations. For improving the quality of human life, a wide variety of medical and assistive devices were developed.

Careers in Biomedical Engineering
ISBN 978-0-12-814816-7
https://doi.org/10.1016/B978-0-12-814816-7.00003-0

About 3000 years ago, unsung Egyptian biomedical engineer developed a wooden prosthetic body part, which was discovered with one of mummies near Luxor in Egypt (Finch et al., 2012). It was assumed not only just cosmetic prosthetic but also used as for supporting to walk. It was clear that Egyptian engineer tried to replace missing body part by commonly available materials and help amputee to regain the freedom of mobility. The design of prosthetic would not be based on the science and engineering theories, but it was obvious that the creator carefully observed a human foot and replicated its functionality.

Curiosity to see and represent the object has always been a major driving factor in the biomedical engineering history. Eyeglasses are another example of biomedical engineering, which is an instrument for correcting distorted human vision, to clearly see the world. Development of optics and lenses created a compound microscope, which opened the door to explore a cell and its movement. Enhancing the power of observation pushed a simple microscope to much higher magnification using electron by which the digital technologies have been enhanced. The nuclear imaging technique was also introduced and has been used in current medical practice to observe the inside of human body without dissection. Static imaging (i.e., X-ray image) is now more dynamic and complex imaging process (i.e., functional MRI). From small to large scale, from clear to precise, and from static to dynamic, biomedical engineer utilized engineering skills to diverse and accelerate the life science researches more.

The term of biomedical engineering started to be used in the late 1950s. During this period, many professional societies were established and started their own communication platforms. The IEEE Engineering in Medicine and Biology Society (EMBS, established in 1952) started the Transactions of Biomedical Engineering (formally IRE Transactions on Medical Electronics) in 1955 (Greatbatch and Castle, 1955), the Biomedical Engineering Society (BMES, established in 1968) started the Annals of Biomedical Engineering in 1972 (Lyman and Yates, 1972), and the American Society of Mechanical Engineers (ASME) started the Journal of Biomechanical Engineering in 1977 (Brighton, 1977). Because the Biomedical Engineering has been consisted by the multidisciplinary life science and engineering fields, the material part of the biomedical engineering started the Biomaterials in 1980 (Bruck and Hastings, 1016). These historical milestones indicate that the biomedical engineering substantially expanded after 1960s, and it is now still expanding its field for advancing the quality of human life.

In 1976, the United States Congress passed the Medical Device Amendments (Public Law 94-295) to the Federal Food, Drug, and Cosmetics Act. After that, the Safe Medical Devices Act and further amendments were made, to make sure that any new medical devices after 1990 were safe to be used. This occurred as part of the FDA approval processes, which dramatically bolstered requirements for the biomedical engineering world. Many unsafe and scientifically suspicious medical devices were naturally weeded out from the major market.

On the other hand, the approval process ensured the safety of the device, and unique innovative products, which had not fully proved functionality and safety, became more difficult to be introduced in the market. In addition, the approval process requires a wide variety of testing and verification processes, which requires time, human resources, and financial viability. It is expected that next generation of biomedical engineering will be more complex and diverse than current one. Requirements for the biomedical engineer will be more challenging than ever. The trend in the biomedical engineering has been swaying between large and small scales: for example, from the human factor biomechanics to cellular-level biomechanics. Both the business and education sectors, especially Science, Technology, Engineering, and Math (STEM) education, will play a significant part of the future biomedical engineering development.

TYPES OF POSITIONS AND CAREERS AVAILABLE

Traditionally, biomedical engineers are categorized by discipline—separated into groups of specialties such as bioinstrumentation, biomaterials, biomechanics, systems physiology, medical imaging, and clinical engineering. Bioinstrumentation is the designing and developing of tools and equipment that are used to diagnose and treat diseases. Biomaterials include the design and development of materials that are suitable for use within the human body. Biomaterials includes analyzing materials for the safety of patients (biocompatibility); the stability of material (chemical makeup and leveraging the outcomes); or cellular, tissue, and genetic engineering. Biomechanics includes analysis of body motion and products that aid with motion within the body. Systems physiology includes understanding on how organisms function and working on the organism level. Medical imaging includes all the engineering and science that is used in imaging technologies. And finally, there is clinical engineering that involves people working in hospitals and health care facilities to find uses for medical products

(Top Master's in Healthcar, 2018). It should be noted that categorizing biomedical engineering into specialties in this way is challenging in that many of these fields overlap, new categories and fields are being invented continually, and some of these topics are very broad and encompass many different specialties and aspects.

Biomedical engineers can work in many different settings. On the research and development side, engineers can work in universities, hospitals, start-ups, original equipment manufacturers (OEMs), and contract research consultancies. In the manufacturing and maintenance of devices, biomedical engineers can work in hospitals, start-ups, large multinational OEMs, medium-sized OEMs, start-ups, contract manufacturing, and/or testing facilities. Just as in other fields, many companies are global and virtual with ample opportunities to collaborate with global teams and for travel.

As discussed earlier, biomedical engineering requires a background in an engineering discipline, but it also requires an integration of additional concepts, such as human body reaction, quality systems, and regulatory. Most biomedical engineers start their career with an excellent education in an engineering discipline and some knowledge of human body science in the form of anatomy and/or physiology. They have a high comfort level with technical knowledge learned in school; however, their knowledge of how a device is developed is rather limited. Topics such as quality management systems (QMS), design control, regulatory, and change control are sometimes skimmed over in traditional education and instead are focused on during on-the-job training. Integration of these topics is critical to a person's success in biomedical engineering. The first thing any new employee must do when joining a medical device company is to learn the standard operating procedures (SOPs), which are the procedures that govern all the activities in the company, so they can be assured that the company and its employees follow FDA regulations. Every engineer needs a basic understanding of QMS and work under the company's SOPs.

A company's QMS incorporates FDA regulatory requirements as well as ISO (International Organization for Standardization) standards that outline good design, testing, and manufacturing practices. The SOPs guide employees in developing, designing, testing, and manufacturing safe and effective products that will pass muster with FDA regulators. Companies have the freedom to develop policies and practices that meet their individual needs but still adhere to the FDA and ISO standards. The regulations and standards apply to all companies, leading to SOPs that have much in common form company to company. Specific areas all

SOPs cover include requirements management (how to determine what is being designed and what standards should the outcome be tested to), risk management (what can go wrong and how to mitigate errors), verification and validation activities (how to know if the final product meets requirements), and change control (how to ensure consistency of the final product over time).

In biomedical engineering, discovering, developing, designing, manufacturing, and commercialization of medical products require a cross-functional team working together through the product life cycle. Some common titles of biomedical engineers include

- Manufacturing Engineer
- Quality Engineer
- System Engineer
- Researcher
- Scientist
- Physician
- Regulatory Engineer
- Development/Principle Engineer/Software Engineer/Hardware Engineer
- Project or Program Manager
- Technical Sales Manager

Regardless of the type of the device, there is a common cycle for development, and each of the functions below has an important role in bringing the device to market. The medical product cycle (Fig. 3.1) includes the following steps:

1. Research
2. Design and Development (D&D)
3. Testing
4. Manufacturing
5. Regulation
6. Commercialization
7. Maintenance.

Developing a medical product begins with research. The engineers who work in research at the beginning of the cycle are looking to discover new medical products or new applications for existing technology. Once the "idea" or technology and potential application are established, the discovery team engages with the design and development team to develop official requirements for the medical product. Requirements are the foundation of designing and building a device—a requirement under FDA regulations—and a fundamental part of the market success of the product. At a high level,

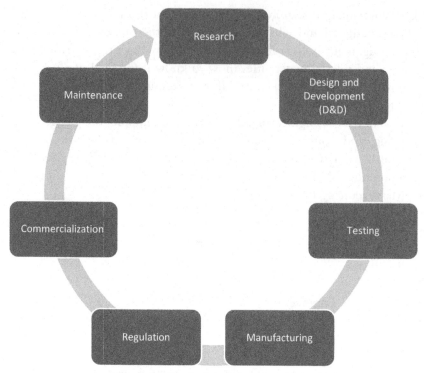

Figure 3.1 Medical device product cycle.

the regulations mandate that the medical device has defined requirements that detail what a successful product will look like.

Then, engineers design to those requirements, test the device to the requirements, and develop systems to control consistency in achieving the requirements in manufacturing. After the research step has defined the product and has started to define the requirements, the design and development team finalizes the market or high-level requirements, translates them into functional requirements and specifications, designs the product, and produce the documents that guide building the device and all of its components. During the development portion, test engineers provide intermediate feedback on how well the team is meeting the requirements. After the design is finalized, the verification and validation activities performed by test engineers determine whether the device design meets the requirements. Once the team has completed the testing to show that they meet the requirements, manufacturing engineers develop processes to ensure that devices can be built repeatedly over time and as production levels increase troubleshoot issues that occur with increased volume in manufacturing. Regulation activities typically involve a third-party review and audit to approve the device for use. The regulatory reviews happen internally within the company, sometimes involving a third-party review by a private company, and, in most cases, reviewed by FDA. Commercialization involves the sales, marketing, and distribution departments that provide access to the product after FDA approval. And, finally, maintenance of the device includes activities that ensure that the product is undergoing maintenance and calibration activities to meet intended performance criteria as well as to track issues and defects of products in the field.

To consider how biomedical engineers interrelate throughout the development cycle of a medical product provides insight into roles and responsibilities of the engineers in their own habitat. Furthermore, an individual career can be entirely within one of these categories (i.e., research, design and development, etc.) or can be defined by a specialty, such as orthopedics, imaging, or neurostimulation, that crosses multiple stages of device development. Experiences also differ based on the size of any company, complexity of the device(s), number of devices under development, and other factors; these functions can be segmented between multiple people or combined under the list of duties for one employee. For example, in a large, multinational, medical device, product company, each stage in the development lifecycle will be represented by one or more individuals during the development: there is a whole department of test engineers, an entire department of process engineers, a comprehensive department of manufacturing engineers, and a complete department of sustaining manufacturing engineers. On the other hand, in a small start-up of 10 people, the same engineer might be designing the product, performing tests, developing the manufacturing processes, and taking out the garbage. There are also companies that specialize in supporting medical device companies on a contract or consulting basis. For example, a company may specialize in electrical safety testing, and they have a team of engineers that focus on one specific type of testing for the product developer. Other examples include contract design firms, contract development firms, contract research firms, other contract testing services, regulatory consultants, and contract manufacturers.

In the following sections, each category of medical device development will be discussed in terms of the positions and duties that are needed to develop a successful device.

Research

Medical devices start as an invention or discovery. As in any field, discovery or invention can happen in a clinical setting, in a laboratory, research facility, by general observation in the field, or anywhere innovation can happen. Examples of where discoveries can come from are

- a practitioner finding a solution to an unsolved or poorly solved problem;
- a technological savvy person who recognizes an application of a new technology;
- a researcher leveraging market research and knowledge of the field through years of involvement and return on investment (ROI) analysis to identify an opportunity;
- an individual looking at a clinical or human problem from a unique perspective; and
- a person applying their years of education and experience from an adjacent field into medical devices.

These opportunities typically start out like most initial ideas with a very small group of dedicated individuals chasing an idea. Examples include a small seed project in a large multinational OEM that is trying to evaluate a need and feasibility, a clinician teaming up with an engineer who believes in a concept, or a person who is entrepreneurial in the technology space and sees the possibility of applying that technology to the human body who teams up with a biomedical engineer. But no matter how they are initiated, they start small with developing the technology, confirming discoveries and seeking funding—either through grants, internal review boards, and/or seed and angel funding.

After the initial idea starts to show promise for an application, the team starts to grow and the idea is stressed or tested, and questions are asked:

Does this idea have merit?

Is the idea technically sound?

Is there a need in the market place?

Is there a value in the marketplace?

What is the competition?

Is it novel?

Can it be designed to be safe?

What regulatory path would be best?

What will the team look like?

What skill sets are needed to develop the concept?

What are the risks?

What does success look like?

How much money and time will it take to fully develop and release it into the market?

What IP, intellectual property, is available to protect this idea?

To answer these questions, the team members shift focus from discovery to development of their idea. The skill sets needed as the idea grows is a combination between a deep knowledge and expertise in the technical field and business knowledge and market familiarity as well as ability to develop the business case (ROI in the large company) or ability to raise fund through grants or seed funding in the small company case. These skill sets translate into technology expertise, engineering, marketing, regulatory, and business savvy. The goal of this stage is to quickly identify if the idea will be able to move forward into a marketable and profitable product, identify the risks, identify the development plan, identify the time and cost, and identify the return on the investment. Additionally, people are needed with experience to provide insights into the "how"—how will this idea become a reality. The members of the team are required to have the capability in hypothesis and test method development, grant writing/fundraising, project management, research, making connections, and partnering. In a larger company with multiple products, the research team will then start to add team members. The core team includes the originator of the idea in the researcher/scientist/clinician(s), a principle engineer(s), and project manager.

Regulatory expertise, marketing expertise, intellectual property (IP) expertise, other engineering expertise, test engineer, and maybe even a manufacturing engineer are all brought in as needed during this phase to develop the strategy. In a small start-up, the team might still be a researcher/scientist/physician, an engineer, and a business savvy person, but they might look to contractors, consultancies, and service providers to fill in any gaps in their capabilities. At this stage, engaging with and intellectual property lawyer, marketing research firm, regulatory firm, strategy consultants, and even starting conversations with contract design and development firms to get budgetary estimates prior to fundraising are all possible partners the team might interface with to gain the necessary knowledge and perspective.

If there is a desire to build a company around the new technology and device development, the team forms an entity around the discovery, seeks out IP, and seeks out grant or seed/angel funding. In a new company, they will also need to determine how they will meet the quality control requirements for the next stage design and development regulation. The company might choose to develop a QMS internally or look to a contract organization to fulfill this need. They need quality engineering representation either way to develop or oversee the QMS.

Not all research will lead to medical products. Biomedical engineers might stay in the research mode for their entire careers. They help clinicians develop therapies and provide information for diagnoses in clinical settings. In laboratory and university settings, they provide information and data for the purpose of moving knowledge forward and publishing without the end goal of a final product in mind. In the university model, the research team's goal is to expand knowledge through publishing, so if they are able to develop a marketable technology, they would probably "spin out" the idea into a small company or license the technology to another group.

Design and Development

Design and development (D&D) is the act of turning technology into a product. Once the overall strategy and ROI are determined, the project has funding and/or approved budget and plan, device development and design can begin.

The engineering team in the D&D stage expands into of all the appropriate disciplines for the device, which can be a broader subset than just the technology team. For example, if the product is electromechanical, even though the technology development was only mechanical, the team will consist of biomedical engineers with backgrounds in mechanics, electrical engineering, software engineering (most likely), and materials engineering. If the product is a mechanical implant with a new material, such as a hip replacement implant, the team will consist of materials engineers who understand the new technology and mechanical engineers to help turn the technology into a product but probably would not need electrical and software engineering. In addition to the engineering team, the product team needs inputs from clinical or medical representatives, human factors engineer, quality engineer, project manager, packaging engineer, etc. The research team is critical to ensure that the baseline technology is developed properly and reduce errors in translation. Additionally, the team could require inputs from the test engineer, process or manufacturing engineer, human factors engineering, industrial designers, regulatory engineers or representatives, and marketing or sales representatives.

The first step for the team is to flesh out the requirements. In the research stage, the team focused on the user and market requirements and the requirements specific to the technology focus. These requirements need to be brought together and expanded on in this stage in order to gain a full understanding of the intended final product. To do this, the technical team works with the regulatory team and quality team to identify applicable standards that provide insight as to standards and testing required for a specific type of device. Additionally, the team begins the risk analysis by identifying hazards for the device and areas of misuse or failure at the device and user level. Identifying the risks provide further insight into where requirements are needed to safeguard the device. Proof of concept models and engineering test models are often developed at this point to work through design concepts and narrow in on additional requirements. These proof of concepts can generate user feedback and provide information in usability and human factors that are inputs for risk analysis and requirements definition.

Once the requirements are set, the team then works on turning the initial requirements and proof of concept design into device specifications and design. This process is typically iterative and cycles through various prototypes as the device design matures. As the design transitions from alpha to beta prototypes and beyond, the team pulls in the appropriate skill sets from test engineers to put together the test plan for V&V (verification and validation). The test plan is based on showing that the engineering team can meet each requirement. Each version of the prototype is used to gain confidence that the final V&V testing will be successful with smaller versions of similar tests.

In larger companies, this team is pulled together from various departments to support the program or project manager in developing the device. A member of the team can be dedicated or be partially supporting many different product development initiatives depending on the project needs, person, skill sets, etc. In smaller companies, there is a focus on only one product at a time, and they could have the resources on hand to fill the project needs with different individuals. The small start-up typically hires a core team of multidisciplinary people to piece together the core functions as necessary and supplements as needed with temporary help. Typical positions and skill sets in the core team are systems engineering, project management, engineering representative from the core technology (i.e., if a mechanical device a biomechanical engineer), and quality and regulatory engineer. This core team takes on the same tasks in both large and small companies but in small companies and start-ups they take on more multidisciplinary roles. For example, the biomechanical engineer in a small start-up might be responsible for scoring the regulations for applicable standards, leading the risk assessment activities, developing the test plans, performing testing, and designing the device.

Where the team's skill sets need supplementing (in both large and small companies), the team looks to hire contract or consulting services. A consultant interfaces as an individual contributor to the team, while a contract service provider is typically treated more as a "supplier" to the technical team and has a different level of responsibility and deliverables. Some common areas for hiring a service provider at this stage are industrial design, regulatory, design, testing, usability and human factors but can be any function that there is a need. There are also contract service providers who provide all design and development services so the small and nimble 2–3 person start-up company might not ever need to hire more than a couple of engineers to help oversee the development.

Engineers working for a contract service provider have the same functions as if they worked for a large or small company. In many cases, the contract service provider mirrors all the positions as the device developer. The benefit of hiring these groups is there is access to experts in very specific areas of device design and development without the overhead of full time hires or the burden of finding individual consultants. For the engineers employed at these types of organizations, there are many benefits and shortcomings. Benefits include being able to see and work with a number of different projects, being able to see a huge cross-section of medical devices, different technologies, applications, patients, customers, etc. This keeps everyday new and different and allows for a very diverse work environment daily, weekly, and yearly. Additionally, working for the contract service providers allows the engineer to become an expert in a specific area of device development with a lot of practice in a narrow area. On the downside, there is a large expectation of customer service because the service provider is on a fee for service contract. Additionally, there is a lack of ownership of the products that are assigned as once the contract is over; many OEM's move on from their contract partners after the specific scope of work is completed.

Testing

The goal of the testing phase is to prove out of the technology for safety and effectivity and to ensure the device meets the requirements and standards identified in the earlier stages. As discussed earlier, it is prudent to initiate some of the testing during the design and development phase, but the verification and validation (V&V) testing shows that the device reliably (with statistical significance) meet the requirements and regulations and that the device is safe and effective. The V&V test results are an important part of the packet that is submitted to the FDA as evidence that the device is ready to be sold to and used by the general medical community.

Testing challenges all aspects of the device from the perspective of electrical, software, body response/chemical, mechanical, so the engineering inputs from the core technical team is still required. In addition to the core team contributions, the quality engineering function becomes more critical, and the manufacturing engineer and regulatory engineer both begin to get involved.

In addition to previous segments, the engineering work in this phase requires knowledge of statistics and verification and validation principles and test method verification. The test engineer's responsibility is to fully develop the test plan based on the requirements and standards and to execute the testing required. The engineers need to able to research applicable standards to find standard test methods, write or modify test methods as needed (test methods that are new or modified off the standard will require test method validation and/or rationale as to why they needed to be modified), use good scientific principles to write test protocols, have the test executed (or execute the test themselves), and finally analyze the data and draw conclusions that will be documented various reports. Analysis of the data is typically required to be statistically significant or be justified, so a working knowledge of statistics is needed. The quality and regulatory team supports this activity because the results need to be written up and provided for the FDA approval of the device.

Again, there are specialized companies that will provide testing and risk management services or the company can complete the testing internally. Using a testing service enables the device developer access to experts and needed equipment to complete testing in an efficient manner. For engineers working in these firms, contract testing service providers allow engineers to follow specialized career paths in testing services, such as electrical safety, software testing, mechanical testing services, biocompatibility testing, animal testing, and clinical engineering testing. Additionally, this allows engineers with specific interest in testing to develop significant depth as a test engineer in their chosen field.

Another aspect of testing the device includes clinical, field, or animal trials. These tests occur for various purposes. They can be to gain insight from the user group as part of the human factors engineering, the tests can be to gain insight to the effectivity of the device, to gain insights into the risks, or to inform details in preparing the accompanying instructions that might be needed. From the perspective of human factors and usability, the testing is in the form of formative and summative tests with user groups where impressions and errors from the end user groups are collected. Efficacy is typically tested in animals and/or clinical trials. Good testing practices and test method development are required to ensure that the data are not skewed or lead to erroneous conclusions (either accidentally or purposefully). Statistical methods are again an important part as well as technical writing of protocols, test cases, reports, etc. Being able to read and interpret standards are also critical here as well as the technical acumen to interpret the data collected—so clinical knowledge is critical. In some cases, behavioral science approach to questionnaires will be needed to ensure that the user groups provide unbiased feedback.

Testing can be engineering level, verification level, or validation level. Verification testing indicates whether the functional requirements and specifications have been met, and validation activities testing indicate whether user requirements have been met. Validation testing is more typically clinical in nature looking at the device holistically; either clinical testing itself or reliable replacements for clinical tests, while verification and engineering testing happens on the benchtop or laboratory and occur in a more focused isolated manner looking at discrete pieces of the whole product.

Manufacturing

Manufacturing can occur at the team's facility or in a contract manufacturing setting. The device developer uses a litmus based on risk and cost to determine which strategy is beneficial to the company: does the benefit of developing the capability of manufacturing the device in house outweigh the efficiencies of using a contract manufacturing partner? However, even if the team decides to use in house facilities, there will be some outsourcing required in materials, components, or subassembly purchases.

Manufacturing input in medical devices starts in the early alpha prototype stages where the prototype manufacturing is used to provide feedback to the design (term called design for manufacturing; DFM). Prototype assembly can occur at specialized prototype assemblers or on equipment at the manufacturing partner or internally.

Manufacturing of medical devices requires a very controlled setting utilizing good manufacturing practices (GMP) and follows ISO 13485 principles and approaches, but the facility is typically certified to ISO 13485. Additionally, manufacturers and contract manufacturers are required to register with the FDA. Similar to nonmedical manufacturing, there is expectation of minimizing error and maximizing quality. Ideally, manufacturing engineers have input throughout the process from design and development and into the testing portions of the previous sections to ensure that the final product can be manufactured consistently in the most efficient manner available.

Manufacturing engineers along with process engineers and sustaining manufacturing engineers are responsible for producing reproducible processes for building medical devices, whether that involves automation or very manual processes, there has to be the demonstration of control. Quality inspection is a very large part of manufacturing and will require the quality engineer to work hand in hand with the manufacturing engineers to ensure of high-quality output. A strong grasp of lean manufacturing concepts, technical writing, and statistics are paramount in being successful in manufacturing-related positions. Additionally, the manufacturing engineers will use risk analysis to inform about where in the process things can go wrong and introduce risks to the users. These areas will require additional testing and scrutiny during the development of the process, during the testing of the manufacturing process, and the additional testing will be worked into the manufacturing process itself once finalized.

Engineers in medical device manufacturing can be split into two categories: setting up manufacturing lines and maintenance of the manufacturing lines. In many cases, these two responsibilities can overlap, but in larger companies that have more specialized roles, these can be separate positions. In addition, management of the production technicians and operators is typically a separate job path.

Setting up manufacturing lines typically includes input to design for manufacturability to ensure that the design chosen can be build. Not all design engineers design devices that can be built due to limitations caused materials, physics, or available manufacturing processes that may not be apparent when an engineer is working solely in design models. Other aspects for design for manufacturing include making design choices that will maximize reliability and the ability to manufacture predictable outcomes and minimize errors. Additional considerations will include identifying key points for inspections as determined during risk analysis and the ability to design processes that are scalable.

After working with the design team for DFM input, a manufacturing engineer or process engineer will start designing the process for the manufacturing of components and final assembly of the device. They will address questions, such as what order is best for assembly, inspection, and reliability; what processing methods are optimal (for example, if addressing the connection of two wires: should the wires be soldered, glued with conductive glue, or crimped to their connections); what parameters for the process and equipment are optimal to meet design requirements and what are the limits to these parameter; what is the repeatability of these outcomes given the variability in the parameters; what suppliers should be chosen; and how will the manufacturer evaluate quality of the supplied components or assemblies. Similar to the design and development testing activities, the manufacturing and quality engineers will need to conduct verification and validation tests to show that the manufacturing specifications are met and that these specifications reliably meet the underlying requirements. The manufacturing engineers during this period will interface extensively with the core design team, the purchasing department, quality engineering, regulatory engineering, and testing engineering.

Once the device passes all the rigors of reliability and repeatability from a production perspective, it can be "released" into full production mode. As with typical production scenarios key process indicators and checkpoints for requirements are monitored for patterns of failures; defects, and excess scrap, anomalies in production statistics are monitored, tracked, and troubleshoot; then, continuous improvement activities are ongoing. Any recommended changes after a certain point is under strict change control and possibly require FDA submission and approval before official change is permitted. The manufacturing engineers will work with the team as part of the "maintenance" activities to troubleshoot field issues and quality issues that occur.

Regulation

During the entire design and development process through manufacturing, the medical device companies need to exhibit control over the design and development process and any changes after verification and validation. Internally, the design and development companies as well as their contractors and service providers are required to work within 21 CFR and ISO 13485 guidelines. These are standards and regulations for the design and development process and change control that are controlled by each company's QMS. In addition, to setting up the systems and following them, companies are required to internally audit their systems. This is typically organized by the quality team; however, they can recruit many different individuals to act as auditors as long as there is an objectiveness to the investigator, typically someone who is not directly involved with that particular function/requirement. Supplier audits also fall into this category. Supplier audits are like internal audits, where the device developer is expected to show control of their processes and inputs to the medical device. The supplier audits are performed by the hiring company's quality engineering department typically, but it can be a multidisciplinary team also.

Auditing requires an extreme level of attention to detail. It requires extensive knowledge of the requirements and regulations and the ability to quickly and thoroughly understand the intricacies of the policies and procedures of a company, as well as be very detailed oriented. There is a type of comradery that can be built with the auditee—one of the improvements— but often there is an animosity between the two parties.

In addition, all systems are then subject to review and periodic audit by a third-party-notified body. This is a private company hired by the device developer to audit and provide certification of compliance to the standards. Biomedical engineers, additionally, can work at these third-party companies to work with their clients to maintain compliance. The third party does this through auditing, reviewing, providing education, and in some cases approving submissions.

A small subset of engineers with expertise in this area can also work at the FDA itself. At the FDA, there are opportunities to audit and review documentation packages, to be the technical expert when devices come up for review, review feedback from devices in the field, and to work on policy and new standards and regulations to improve safety and effectiveness of medical devices and the approval and monitoring of the devices.

Commercialization

All around the medical device development world, there are many jobs and careers that help support the industry. Many of these positions are perfect for the engineer who wants to try something new, but still leverage their technical knowledge. Additionally, these careers are a great way of people with alternative backgrounds to enter the field.

Sales

Medical device sales are a highly competitive industry. It offers high compensation with a high level of autonomy. In many cases, sales in a medical device manufacturer or developer setting is the interface with the doctors and surgeons who help advise on the appropriate products, offer a level of training in some cases, and provide feedback to the device developer. Some medical device sales individuals can end up in surgical sweets and are potentially even on call for when their device will be utilized.

Selling also occurs on the level of each contract manufacturer, supplier, auditing or notifying body, test house, etc. Each of these sales representatives to be successful should have the ability to understand the capabilities and technical benefits of the team and typical sales skills that come with any sales position. In some cases, there are teams of sales personnel where one tracks down leads, one builds the relationship, and one more technical sales manager will be brought in to discuss the opportunity from a specific technical standpoint and develop the proposal or quotation. Technical sales representatives require an engineering degree and some direct experience and/or training in the specific technology being sold.

Marketing

Marketing is similar in medical devices as in other industries. Marketing must be able to work hand in hand with the technical team during the development cycle to be successful. The ability to identify and adjust the technology from the perspective of the target market is paramount in designing the device for the appropriate market. For example, a device used only in a research hospital setting may have very different requirements and look very different with different features than a device that is designed to work in the home. While marketing is typically its own employment path, for biomedical engineers with extensive knowledge of a market segment, there are opportunities to step out of the technical contributor role into a marketing role with the advantage of understanding the technology behind the products.

Maintenance

Maintenance of the medical device can fall into three categories: maintenance of the device failure log and feedback to manufacturers, maintenance of the devices in the final setting, and the training and continued support of the distribution and sales process.

The FDA requires analysis of field failures that gets submitted both to the FDA and back to the manufacturer to minimize field failures and injury caused by devices. Extensive efforts are put into troubleshooting returns, categorizing them, and determining root cause. The core technical engineering team will typically assist the manufacturing engineers to troubleshoot and determine root cause of any issues. Quality engineers help monitor these activities, and regulatory engineers help determine the extent of change required and if necessary are involved in submitted changes and recalls to the FDA.

Most people without a biomedical engineering background assume that the only thing biomedical engineers maintain equipment in the hospital. While the breadth of Biomedical Engineer's opportunities are much broader than this, there are people who are needed to maintain hospital and clinical equipment. In maintenance, they typically are tasked with following and keeping track of the various maintenance and calibrations of the medical equipment. Just as the processes in medical device development and manufacturing are highly controlled, it is as important for the safety of the patients that the equipment is maintained and calibrated properly.

Finally, proper use of the devices is very important. Training of physicians may happen from the sales team but can also be completed via a specialized training group to ensure that physicians and clinicians are using their devices properly. Additionally, training can take on many forms to help inform companies along the value chain about the regulations and requirements as well as keeping everyone updated on the continually shifting landscape.

Project Management

One of the most challenging positions in medical device development in the program or project management position. This person typically has a combination of technical skills, organization skills, management skills, budgeting skills, and communication skills. The program manager is responsible to keep the project on time line and budget and communicate progress to all stakeholders. Most project managers are intimate with the technical details of the project to understand and plan for any issues that will arise during the development. A technical background is recommended as well as a general understanding of all the individual inputs to the device as the program manager will be required to guide individuals of the team during crises and communicate intelligently. A project manager can also have a project management certification, but certification is typically only required in the largest organizations.

Most medical devices are developed with a project-based approach, which leads to a matrix organization or a hierarchy dependent on the specific project. This means that the project manager often has management responsibility of the team members. They should be trained as managers or have managerial experience if the hierarchy is based on projects or if in a matrix organization the program engineers needs to be proficient in "influencing without authority." The ability of the program manager to motivate and effectively direct their team as well as managing the schedule and budget is the difference between success or failure.

EDUCATION AND TRAINING

To become a biomedical engineer or to work in the biomedical engineering field, pursuing academic degrees can be the most reliable steps. Many academic institutions are accredited by the Accreditation Board for Engineering and Technology (ABET), which assures the academic institution demonstrates the quality of engineering education. In addition, the students who graduated from the accredited school imply that they will be able to utilize gained knowledge as for an engineer. Depending on the degree levels, the career pathways will be different. Fig. 3.2 represents conceptual academic degree differences in the biomedical engineering. During the undergraduate level toward the bachelor's degree, students are required to study mathematics, physics, chemistry, biology, and engineering classes. The field of biomedical engineering consists of a wide variety of science and engineering disciplines. Therefore, biomedical engineering students are expected to have much broader fundamental knowledge of both life science and engineering.

Advancement of the academic degree is an opportunity to seek further comprehension of the biomedical engineering. Higher level of research-based education expands fundamental knowledge into more focused biomedical engineering discipline. For example, the field of biomechanics can be specialized as cellular, bone, joint, material, rehabilitation, occupational, or human factor, which serves more specific biomechanical applications. In addition, most of these advanced degree programs require to conduct independent research activities. Students are required to develop their own research plan and to present their progress professionally to peers. This may be different from corporate research and development processes, but students are trained to conduct their hands-on activities logically. This is a

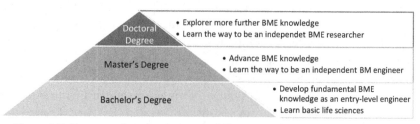

Figure 3.2 Conceptual academic degree differences in biomedical engineering.

training to be an independent biomedical engineer or researcher in the specific field of biomedical engineering.

Not only the degree process but also the academic institution needs to be carefully considered for the biomedical engineering education and training. Selection of the degree program can be done by name of school, size, faculty to student ratio, quality of education, history of reputation, future career paths, and so on. However, this is not so well informed that the degree program has a unique history of establishment within the school. Many undergraduate biomedical engineering programs try to cover majority of biomedical engineering contents. However, because the biomedical engineering is newer engineering field, the faculty members were trained in traditional engineering categories, such as the mechanical, electrical, chemical, or civil engineering. As seen in Fig. 3.2, this fact leads some biomedical engineering programs are originated from the mechanical engineering, which could emphasize on the biomechanics, biofluid, bionics, rehabilitation engineering, orthopedic bioengineering, and so on. When the program is more leaning to the electrical and computer engineering, which could focus on biomedical electronics, biomechatronics, bioinstrumentation, medical imaging, systems physiology, neural engineering, bioinformatics, clinical engineering, and so on. In addition, if the biomedical engineering program is based on the chemical, biological, and/or material sciences, which could shift to the biomaterials, cellular, tissue, genetic engineering, bionanotechnology, and so on. The biomedical engineering field is dynamic and flexible, so these subcategories are getting hybrid between each other. This is another reason that the biomedical engineering requires to have extremely wider range of science and engineering knowledge (Fig. 3.3).

Historically, the engineering education in the university level more focuses on the theoretical aspects with supplemental hands-on laboratory activities. This has been used as necessary pedagogy to explain the complex engineering concepts from fundamental to advanced levels. However, traditional university education might impress students that it does not prepare well to face the demands of job market. Many engineering companies desire to hire flexible, skillful, knowledgeable, and highly motivated engineers. Especially, the biomedical engineering companies are willing to hire new engineer to be placed in one of following: (1) research, (2) design and development, (3) testing, (4) manufacturing, (5) auditing and FDA approval, and (6) selling, marketing, and maintenance of device. Therefore, it is significantly important to have a series of design

Biomedical Engineering	Mechanical Engineering	Biomechanics
		Biofluid
		Bionics
		Rehabilitation Engineering
		Orthopaedic Bioengineering
	Electrical and Computer Engineering	Biomedical Electronics
		Biomechatronics
		Bioinstrumentation
		Medical Imaging
		Systems Physiology
		Neural Engineering
		Bioinformatics
		Clinical Engineering
	Biological, Chemical, Material Sciences	Biomaterials
		Cellular and Tissue Engineering
		Genetic Engineering

Figure 3.3 Areas of biomedical engineering and traditional science and engineering categories.

classes from first year to fourth year of curriculums. The freshmen to junior-level design classes are typically semester long to experience the engineering design processes from beginning of brainstorming to final product. The senior design project class tends to be longer and more realistic than early design classes. The senior design class should be the highlight of the university engineering education. It can incorporate financial and/or six-sigma–oriented design consideration into the brainstorming process. The business analysis, such as target user or market size assessments, can also be discuss and reflect to the design and final prototype. The engineering ethics and social responsibilities can be emphasized in their design, report, and presentations. If the project is aimed for the medical device, this is an excellent example to consider the FDA approval process and its testing mechanisms. In addition, the design process is able to discuss the patent process, as well as the intellectual property topics. These aspects can be explained and discussed during any standard engineering lectures; however, students can dynamically see and recognize important factors through their project and its progress.

Moreover, the senior design class is a clear transition from passive to active learning style, which will be a life-learning tool for their future careers. Most of undergraduate education may be regarded as somewhat "passive"; students attend the class, receive the lecture materials, complete assigned homework, and grade by set rubrics. This passive style significantly influences students that they always wait to be told what they need to do for next. However, when students graduate from the university, they have to proactively educate by themselves when they face any unknown or unsure topics. Therefore, during the senior design class, students are strongly emphasized to proactively seek the information, digest the contents, and feedback to their design and fabrication process. Many students are so get used to the passive style, so they may take sometimes at the beginning of semester, to adapt a new style. However, once they realize the active learning style, they will be able to find the way naturally based on previously learned science and engineering contents. The topic of biomedical engineering is so diverse and complex, so the active learning style is beneficial tool to expand the knowledge.

The active learning style and the desire to become part of a dynamic field with many opportunities attracts many students. Below one Biomedical Engineer describes her attraction and passion for this field that started in college:

> Biomedical engineering caught my attention in my freshman year of college. I was intrigued by its usefulness to study an individual's interaction with their environment. It was the perfect mix of math, science, mechanical engineering and medicine, as well as being non-invasive. Being able to personally interact with the patients, athletes and research subjects was also a large draw to the field for me as I knew spending my days sitting behind a computer or a microscope was not going to work well for me. My current job responsibilities currently stretch far beyond motion capture, and have expanded into many arms of orthopedics and sports medicine research. However, my underlying knowledge of muscular skeletal biomechanics and modeling allows me to contribute to these various projects.
>
> *Erin Garibay*
> *(Senior Lead Research Engineer @ Medical Center)*

CAREER ADVANCEMENT

Starting as a biomedical engineer in a medical device firm one can expect to have a title, such as "mechanical engineer," "software engineer," "development engineer," etc. From the entry-level engineering positions, the next step would be either to focus on a specific technology or aspect of medical devices to step up into increasingly technical positions or to gain experience and then progress into adjacent positions that will provide a broader perspective of the business, skill sets, and technologies. Additionally, the type of company the engineer chooses to work in will provide very different perspectives and opportunities.

An engineer who chooses to focus on a specific technology will be valuable for their depth of experience. Experience and education are critical in developing the knowledge and skill set in this arena. Typical path would be to a "Senior" Engineer, and then finally "Principal" Engineer who would have responsibilities for technology development and possibly a team of similar engineers working under them looking to the principle engineer for guidance, mentorship, etc.

An engineer who looks to adjacent positions for a broader perspective may be just as proficient or educated but chooses a different path than that of the principle engineer. These folks often find themselves moving into quality or regulatory positions, program management, sales or marketing, etc.

Regardless of the chosen path furthering education is highly regarded in biomedical engineering. Furthering traditional education in achieving a master's degree or PhD in the chosen field shows dedication and a depth of understanding in fundamentals that is valued in the field. Any technical degrees that include a major thesis are also highly regarded as a practical application to classroom work.

Alternatives to furthering a technical education are in furthering education through earning an MBA or similar master's degree in a business field. This line of education is helpful for the engineer who is looking to gain a broader understanding of the business of making medical devices and is seeking an alternative career path.

Additionally, different positions offer many opportunities for on the job training and certifications. For a technical contributor, there are certifications for soldering techniques, computer-aided design work, programming, etc. For quality and regulatory engineers, there are certifications for these positions specifically that are encouraged if not required as part of the training process for these positions. For program managers, there is a project management certification that is often required for attaining a project manager position for a larger medical device company.

One of the largest determining factors for career advancement, however, is what type of company you work for. The experience, perspectives, and opportunities for an engineer in a contract service business is different than those in a large, multinational, medical device developer than those available for an engineer in smaller companies and startup work. Large companies and contract services work tend to allow for more opportunity for specialization because they tend to have positions that focus on very small subsets of the entire development cycle. While small companies tend to require a broader skill set to accommodate a smaller workforce that requires each person to play different roles.

COMPENSATION

From the bureau of Labor Statistics, United States Department of Labor identifies the median pay in 2016 at $85,620 with the lowest 10% earning less than $51,050 and the highest 10% earning more than $134,620 (Greatbatch and Castle, 1955). Compared with other engineering fields, it is typically slightly higher for entry-level salary in that the rigors are slightly higher adding the human studies aspect in training. As with any field, the compensation also differs depending on where in the country the engineer works and the competition for talent in that area. The highest compensation is for principle engineers, senior program managers, and as an engineer enters management in general. Most engineers work on a full-time basis with full benefits: medical, 401k, vacation, and possibly bonuses, profit sharing, etc.

Start-up compensation is more intricate. Based on the stage of start-up, compensation can look just like any other company or it can be a combination of equity shares and direct compensation. In this model, there is obvious downside if the company is not successful in providing value in their medical product. However, there is potential large upside if the device becomes a success. It is a risk that many are willing to take.

FREELANCE OPPORTUNITIES

Medical device development has an abundance of freelance opportunities. The innovative, technical, high growth atmosphere is ripe for experts for hire. There are a few different ways that a company will consider a hiring someone who is freelance. The most popular are

1. strategy consultant
2. technical expert
3. quality and/or regulatory expert
4. troubleshooting expert.

Small companies will eagerly take on freelance workers. They have limited funds at all times and look for ways to minimize overhead. If they can minimize overhead by hiring just the right amount of talent or support, it might cost more per hour, but it saves them from having to hire people for full time, benefits, and not the ability to flex their staff as the product matures through the life cycle, and they need different skill sets. Larger companies will bring in experts to supplement their extensive teams or freshen their skill sets via different perspectives.

Strategy consultants are experienced medical device executives who are hired for specific objectives. It could be to help plan the overall plan for how to get the medical device through FDA clearance or commercialization, or it could be to help a company choose a manufacturing strategy, a device testing strategy, etc. Technical experts are bought in due to a specific technical capability. It could be an expert in one type of medical device technology, such as working with fluid dynamics, working with a specific material, or how a certain aspect of anatomy works. There is a very large market for quality or regulatory experts. Quality and regulatory engineers have a very specialized skill set.

TIPS FOR SUCCESS

To be successful in biomedical engineering, a person needs a strong engineering or technical background, have a passion for helping people, and be able to work in a regulated environment. Many people who get involved with biomedical engineering have a passion for helping people through technology. That passion is the foundation of the most successful engineers and products. Matt Hogan a Senior Project Manager at a large medical device OEM says, "I've always had a love for technology and for improving the lives of people around me. Bioengineering has allowed me to meld those two passions together into a gratifying career. If you want to be a technologist that sees your efforts directly improve the lives of others, it's a rewarding career choice with much potential for growth."

Medical technologies field is currently well behind other fields in the application of cutting edge technology, but there is increased desire and need to accelerate incorporating technology to improve health care in general. Medical devices and solutions of the future will need to be innovative, easy to use, personalized, and incorporate technology that improves medical outcomes and well-being.

Anyone can be successful in medical technologies with passion and hard work. Engineers and technical people interested in the field should not shy away due to lack of experience, education, or anything else. The field needs new perspectives and new ideas to advance, so as long as the individual is willing to work to understand how to develop safe and effective solutions, there are unlimited possibilities.

APPENDICES

Appendix A: Bureau of Labor Statistics—Biomedical Engineers Compensation

Biomedical Engineers
Median annual wages, May 2017
Engineers

$92,220

Biomedical engineers

$88,040

Total, all occupations

$37,690

(Note: All Occupations includes all occupations in the U.S. Economy. Source: U.S. Bureau of Labor Statistics, Occupational Employment Statistics.)

The median annual wage for biomedical engineers was $88,040 in May 2017. The median wage is the wage at which half the workers in an occupation earned more than that amount and half earned less. The lowest 10% earned less than $52,070, and the highest 10% earned more than $142,610.

In May 2017, the median annual wages for biomedical engineers in the top industries in which they worked were as follows (Bureau of Labor Statistic, 2017):

Research and development in the physical, engineering, and life sciences	$95,980
Navigational, measuring, electromedical, and control instruments manufacturing	94,480
Medical equipment and supplies manufacturing	88,190
Health care and social assistance	74,210
Colleges, universities, and professional schools; state, local, and private	61,990

Appendix B: FDA Regulations Overview

FDA Code of Federal Regulations (CFR) Title 21 is the classification of the rules of the FDA pertaining to food and drugs. CFR Title 21 Chapter I, Subchapter H specifically relate to Medical Devices. Subchapter H is broken down into Parts. A sample of the parts in Subchapter H for medical devices are listed below (Code of Federal Regulations – Title 21-Food and Drugs, 2018):

Subchapter H Part	Headings
800	General
801	Labeling
803	Medical device reporting
806	Medical devices: reports of corrections and removals
807	Establishment registration and device listing for manufacturers and initial importers of devices
808	Exemptions from federal preemption of state and local medical device requirements
809	Invitro diagnostic products for human use
810	Medical device recall authority
812	Investigational device exemptions
814	Premarket approval of medical devices
820	Quality system regulation
821	Medical device tracking requirements
822	Postmarket surveillance
830	Unique device identification
860	Medical device classification procedures
861	Procedures for performance standards development
862	Clinical chemistry and clinical toxicology devices
864	Hematology and pathology devices
866	Immunology and microbiology devices
868	Anesthesiology devices
870	Cardiovascular devices
872	Dental devices
874	Ear, nose, and throat devices
876	Gastroenterology-urology devices
878	General and plastic surgery devices
880	General hospital and personal use devices
882	Neurological devices
884	Obstetrical and gynecological devices
886	Ophthalmic devices
888	Orthopedic devices
890	Physical medicine devices
892	Radiology devices
895	Banned devices
898	Performance standard for electrode lead wires and patient cables
1271	Human cells, tissues, and cellular and tissue-based products

References

Brighton, J.A., 1977. Why a journal of biomechanical engineering? Journal of Biotechnology and Engineering 99 (1), 1–2. https://doi.org/10.1115/1.3426262.
Bruck, S.D., Hastings, G., 1995. Editorial, Biomaterials 1 (1), 2. https://doi.org/10.1016/0142-9612(80)90047-2.
Finch, J.L., Heath, G.H., David, A.R., Kulkarni, J., 2012. Biomechanical assessment of two artificial big toe restorations from ancient Egypt and their significance to the history of prosthetics. JPO Journal of Prosthetics and Orthotics 24, 181–191. https://doi.org/10.1097/jpo.0b013e31826f4652.
Greatbatch, W., Castle Jr., J.G., 1955. Forward. IRE Transactions on Medical Electronics (PGME-3) 3. https://doi.org/10.1109/IRET-ME.1955.5008531.
Lyman, J., Yates, F.E., 1972. Editorial, and Annals of Biomedical Engineering 1, 3. https://doi.org/10.1007/BF02363412.
Top Master's in Healthcare Administration, 2018. https://www.topmastersinhealthcare.com/faq/what-types-of-jobs-can-i-get-in-biomedical-engineering/.
Bureau of Labor Statistics, 2017. https://www.bls.gov/ooh/architecture-and-engineering/biomedical-engineers.htm#tab-5.
Code of Federal Regulations – Title 21-Food and Drugs, 2018. https://www.fda.gov/MedicalDevices/DeviceRegulationandGuidance/Databases/ucm135680.htm.

CHAPTER FOUR

Careers in Clinical Engineering

Frank R. Painter
Biomedical Engineering Department, University of Connecticut, Storrs, CT, United States

A career in clinical engineering (CE) is a very good option for an engineer who is interested in being part of the healthcare team. A person in this field becomes the liaison between the clinicians who need and use technology and the developers and manufacturers who provide technology for clinical application and patient care. Medical professionals rely more on technology to monitor, diagnose, and treat their patients and the technology options are more plentiful and complicated than ever. In this kind of a setting, the engineer is a welcome addition to the clinical team helping diagnose and treat patients.

Medical equipment manufacturers are creating more innovative and useful devices for the healthcare environment, yet these devices are also becoming more complicated to manage, implement, connect to other devices, and keep safe. The clinician needs an in-house partner to help select, acquire, install, maintain, and manage these new and evolving technologies. The clinical engineer is the person who is in the best position to do this.

Engineers are usually "systems-thinkers," that is, they approach problems and think about challenges in a different manner than the clinicians, clinical managers, administrators, finance people, or others typically found in the hospital. They bring a different perspective to the table. As a result, they are an excellent and most appreciated addition to the healthcare team. When new equipment is planned, the clinical engineer is part of the committee that determines what is needed. When safety in the hospital is discussed, the clinical engineer is part of the discussion. The clinical engineer is often the project manager for the acquisition of new technology, collaborating with the clinical staff, other departments in the hospital, and the manufacturers/vendors to ensure that the equipment is properly installed and running and the clinicians are trained in its use. The clinical engineers are not expected to be an expert in every aspect, but must be somewhat knowledgeable about most of the technologies in the healthcare environment, giving them the

Careers in Biomedical Engineering
ISBN 978-0-12-814816-7
https://doi.org/10.1016/B978-0-12-814816-7.00004-2

67

obligation and responsibility of almost continuous learning. When unusual problems arise with technology in the patient care environment, rendering the technology potentially hazardous or nonoperational, or when patient injuries occur with the use of medical devices, the clinical engineer often leads the investigation to determine the cause of and resolution to the problem. Clinical engineers may also participate in the design of new medical facilities, providing input on the patient care areas where technology is used. Overall, it is a career that provides a wide variation in day-to-day activities and one that is intellectually stimulating.

BIOMEDICAL ENGINEERING

Clinical engineering is a small segment of the wider specialty of biomedical engineering (BME). Clinical engineering is sometimes known as "applied biomedical engineering." Clinical engineers are sometimes referred to as biomedical engineers, and although technically true, calling them this is a bit misleading. Biomedical engineers are generally involved in the design of medical devices or research related to medical devices. In other words, biomedical engineers are involved very early in the device conception/development process, whereas clinical engineers are involved in maximizing the use of medical devices in the hands of the clinicians. Biomedical engineers are found in academia and working for research, development, and manufacturing firms, whereas clinical engineers are found in the healthcare setting. Clinical engineers use not only engineering principles to understand the technology available for healthcare but also the medical and biological principles on which the device is based, and they use these two sets of information to identify the ideal technology for use at the bedside.

The International Federation of Medical and Biological Engineering and the Imperial College of London define BME as a discipline that advances knowledge in engineering, biology, and medicine and improves human health through cross-disciplinary activities that integrate the engineering sciences with the biomedical sciences and clinical practice. In Wikipedia, BME is simply defined as the application of engineering principles and design concepts to medicine and biology for healthcare purposes (e.g., diagnostic or therapeutic).

The Association for the Advancement of Medical Instrumentation (AAMI) defines a biomedical engineer as a professional with a 4-year or advanced BME degree, who typically works for industry or academia.

The American College of Clinical Engineering (ACCE) defines a clinical engineer as *a professional who supports and advances patient care by applying engineering and managerial skills to healthcare technology.* Clinical engineers manage personnel, finances, instrumentation, and projects to promote the safe and cost-effective application of technology.

AAMI defines a clinical engineer as a professional with a 4-year or advanced engineering degree, who focuses on healthcare technology, typically in a hospital.

HISTORY

Clinical engineering is a fairly new profession. Clinical engineers were in some hospitals prior to the 1970s, but that was mostly to help develop specialized medical equipment for use in the hospital setting. In 1971, Ralph Nader frightened the public and the healthcare industry by stating at least 1200 people per year were electrocuted in needless accidents in hospitals. As a result, electrical safety became an important issue, one that drove the proliferation and advancement of CE. In the same year, Emergency Care Research Institute (ECRI), an organization similar to Consumer Reports but focused on medical devices, published the first monthly issue of the journal, Health Devices, to provide medical equipment evaluations, technology management guidance, and hazard reports focusing on the safety and use of medical equipment. In 1976, the Joint Commission for Accreditation of Hospitals (JCAH, now TJC [The Joint Commission]) caught onto the need for requirements on the quality of medical equipment maintenance and published the first standards related to medical equipment maintenance. This gave the equivalent of a legislative mandate that the CE function be required in hospitals. In the same period, professional certification in CE became available to engineers practicing in the field.

The 1970s was also a time of rapid development in the field of technology management and support in healthcare. The Kellogg Foundation funded more than 10 CE shared services organizations to provide medical equipment maintenance to hospitals across the United States that had not previously had those services from anyone but the manufacturers. From this point on, many quality improvements came from TJC and risk and safety improvements came as a result of the FDA and other's efforts. Medical equipment service innovations and improvements came as a result of service competition among in-house CE programs, independent service organizations, and medical equipment manufacturers' multivendor-based service programs. Today the challenges of CE programs are improving productivity and cost-effectiveness, the demands of changing technologies as equipment becomes more computer based, and managing the risks of larger and more interconnected systems of medical devices.

TYPES OF POSITIONS AND CAREERS AVAILABLE
Positions

The staff clinical engineer is primarily a project manager who must apply BME and management techniques to acquire and implement new technologies. The person in this position is an engineer with a bachelor of science (BS) or sometimes a master of science (MS) degree. This person usually reports to the director of clinical engineering or in a larger hospital perhaps to the manager of clinical engineering who in turn reports to the director. Depending on the education and experience of this person, their salary range would be from $60,000 to $90,000 per year.

A clinical systems engineer is a recent variation of the clinical engineer position. This person is a project manager with a focus on projects related to medical device integration with the electronic medical record. These days, nearly all medical equipment are computer based and capable of passing data about their operation to another computer. Clinical systems engineers design and manage these connections so that the summarized data can be available digitally at the bedside for clinician use. This requires a special expertise in computer networks and data transfer methods. As a result of this additional technical requirement, a person in this position may receive a salary of $65,000 to $100,000 per year.

A medical equipment planner is a clinical engineer who focuses on the medical equipment planning and acquisition process. Medical equipment planners may work for an architectural firm that is planning and building new healthcare facilities or they may work for a large healthcare system that has so many new construction and renovation projects that they need a team dedicated to this function. As you can imagine, the projects this engineer works on are much larger in scope than other CE projects, but the type of work is somewhat narrower in scope than that of a typical clinical engineer. The salary range for this position may be from $50,000 to 80,000 because the educational requirements may be lower in some cases. A clinical engineer is well suited for this position because of their knowledge of medical equipment, the environment in which it is located, and the medical application of the equipment.

In some organizations, clinical engineers may be called medical equipment project managers. This is particularly true if the CE department reports up through the information technology (IT) department. A person in this position will be a combination of a clinical systems engineer and a medical equipment planner and would be paid similar to those positions.

One way for clinical engineers to advance in their career, particularly in salary, would be to, after a period, take on supervisory responsibilities in the department. This may be by supervising people allocated to a project, and it may be assuming management responsibility for a group involved in a particular technical specialty (e.g., laboratory, imaging, surgery) or of groups involved in a specific activity (e.g., maintenance, engineering, planning). In this case a person would advance to the position of clinical engineering supervisor or manager. This position usually requires more experience or additional education than a staff CE position. Correspondingly, the salary would be somewhat larger, at about $75,000–$110,000 per year.

The director of clinical engineering or clinical engineering department head is responsible for setting the direction of the department, for evaluating productivity and cost-effectiveness of the operation, and for growing the program to meet the needs of the healthcare organization. A person in that position usually requires an advanced degree such as a master's degree (MS or master of business administration [MBA]) and several years of experience. They also need to be a leader and someone with a vision of what the department needs to be successful. The salary depends on the geographical area, size of the hospital, and qualifications of the director, but it can range from $85,000 to $150,000 per year.

In a healthcare organization a few clinical engineers advance to the position of chief technology officer. As this person would be working in the ranks of the chief executive officer, chief operation officer, chief financial officer, chief nursing officer, chief information officer, and administrators, it requires an advanced degree in healthcare organizational management. This sounds slightly daunting to some, but the strategic responsibilities of a person in this position can really make an impact on the technology side of healthcare.

Careers

All the positions described so far are found in hospitals and healthcare organizations. The vast majority (greater than 80%) of a clinical engineer's work is as an employee of these organizations. The department of CE will have one or more physical locations in the hospital. Sometimes a larger hospital will provide a "satellite shop" in areas such as the operating room, radiology, respiratory therapy, or the laboratory where there are high concentrations of specialized medical equipment. Other hospitals or hospital systems may have multiple locations where patient care is provided (e.g., outpatient clinics, walk-in centers, smaller hospitals in nearby cities). Most times a "satellite shop" is located there as well. This would be the environment in which an in-house clinical engineer would be based, providing services as needed to all these areas and facilities.

In an in-house program, CE staff are more readily accepted as colleagues by the clinical staff. With everyone being an employee of the same employer, all with a common mission, it is easier to be considered part of the patient care delivery team. Additionally, hospital administrators will more readily listen to requests for funding new activities that benefit the organization if the clinical engineer making the request is an in-house employee. These are the major advantages for clinical engineers, if they are working for a well-run healthcare organization.

Some clinical engineers are employed by very large healthcare systems (e.g., Veterans Administration, Kaiser Permanente, Advent Health). In these systems the clinical engineer's activity is more defined and the direction provided to CE comes from the top of a much larger organization. Employment for competent clinical engineers in this environment is quite stable, so larger employers are preferred by some people.

Many clinical engineers get positions with Independent Service Organizations (ISO) such as TriMedx, Aramark, Sodexo, and Crothall. These organizations sometimes employ clinical engineers in their corporate offices, providing CE resources to a wide number of their clients, but most clinical engineers working for ISO will be employed directly in the hospitals that are customers of the ISO. Many times, the role they assume is the CE manager in the hospital. There are quite a few clinical engineers employed by ISO, perhaps as many as 10%–15% of clinical engineers. Salaries and working conditions for this group are similar to those of in-house employees.

Another mode of employment of clinical engineers is through the manufacturer's multivendor service organizations. Companies such as Philips and GE provide service to hospitals on all medical equipment in the hospital (hence the term multivendor). Most of the time the services provided are just technical services without in-depth CE services, but some larger hospitals have CE services as part of the contract. Many times, just as the ISO would do, the manufacturer will place a clinical engineer as the manager of the CE operation in the hospital. The working environment and work under an employer such as this is very similar to what it would be like working for ISO. Employers like this develop a standardized service delivery model that is used from hospital to hospital, so that a clinical engineer working in this environment would be following a previously developed methodology rather than creating or developing a new approach. One of the advantages of this type of solution is that the hospital will receive a "standard" program that the outside organization will implement and manage for a known fee. This takes the variability and financial risk out of the picture for the hospital and eliminates the hospital having to cope with recruiting and employee performance issues.

A few clinical engineers take positions in equipment planning in an architectural or engineering firm that specializes in building hospitals. This is a very professional work environment, but it involves a lot of travel. If the firm is doing well, this can be a fairly stable work environment. The state of the economy has some influence on the number of hospitals being built at any point in time, but generally, large organizations manage this variability well. One advantage of this type of position is the scope of work the clinical engineer does is narrow enough that the person can become a real expert in the field.

The last career field that will be discussed is taking a position as a clinical engineer for a medical equipment manufacturer assisting in manufacturing and product support. An employer like this may employ clinical engineers to assist in clinical trials of a new prototype of a medical device as it is being developed, before it gets approval by the FDA for marketing to the public. They would do this by taking the product into the clinical environment, observe its use, and report back to the manufacturing and engineering team about the performance of the product so that the design can be adjusted. Clinical engineers may also support the sales group by assisting customers who purchased their medical equipment as it is used in the operating room or other patient care environment in the hospital. These people would function as technical experts on the equipment they are supporting and provide guidance to the hospital staff. They would also provide feedback to the sales or engineering team concerning product performance.

EDUCATION AND TRAINING

The majority of clinical engineers have a BS in engineering. Although many clinical engineers have this degree in BME, an engineering degree in electrical, mechanical, or chemical engineering could suffice. The primary determinant here is does the person think like an engineer and have a desire to work in the clinical environment? Another degree that could be suitable for consideration as a clinical engineer is BS in BME technology. This degree, although at the bachelor's level, has an emphasis on technical aspects. The majority of individuals who receive this degree and end up working in a hospital do so as repair technicians, providing maintenance and repair support to the medical equipment in the hospital. A few do end up with CE responsibilities, but it is not the best degree with which to enter the engineering field.

Many very competent individuals start their careers in the military. In this way they, obtain a very solid educational experience, which is practical and useful, although their training program contains little engineering mathematics and theory. This makes for a very capable technical and management background, but the lack of theory and engineering eventually limits most of these military veterans from CE positions.

For those who want to excel in the CE field an advanced degree is required. Most of the clinical staff in management positions in healthcare organizations have an MS or MBA degree. From a superficial peer recognition point of view, having an MS, MBA, or master of health administration (MHA) degree helps in being accepted as part of the team. Most clinical engineers with advanced education have an MS BME degree. A few have an MS degree in other engineering fields or in science, business, or healthcare administration. The extra training these degrees bring is helpful in almost every respect for clinical engineers.

Many BS BME programs in the United States provide some small orientation to the field of CE. This, however, is usually limited to one or two 1-h classes describing CE responsibilities. Very little education beyond this is provided at the bachelor's level in US schools. Some undergraduate students, who show an interest in CE, may be encouraged to do a volunteer internship in a local hospital. This practical orientation to the field often propels interested students to seek either a job in the field as a clinical engineer or graduate education in CE.

Educational Programs

The primary graduate program in CE in the United States is at the University of Connecticut (UCONN). This 2-year, internship-based MS BME program has been in place for 45 years. The vast majority of its graduates end up in hospitals. Most of the graduate-level courses center around

CE, medical IT, and healthcare technology topics. It is a well-respected program in the CE community, having graduated nearly 150 currently practicing clinical engineers. Two other international graduate CE programs very similar to the UCONN program are at the University of Toronto in Canada and the University of Trieste in Italy.

Another graduate-level program is at the Marquette University. Marquette's Healthcare Technology Management program primarily focuses graduates on working in the manufacturing industry, but some of the graduates have taken CE positions in the hospital setting.

A distance learning program, being offered at the UCONN, provides a master of engineering degree in clinical engineering (MEng CE). This program, which is designed for working professionals, takes about 3 years (10 graduate courses) to complete and can be taken without leaving the job or coming to campus. The prerequisites for this program are a BS degree in engineering or a science and 3 years of CE experience.

Certification

A large number of clinical engineers seek "Certification in Clinical Engineering." The program, which is administered by the Healthcare Technology Certification Commission (HTCC) and sponsored by the ACCE, provides certification for clinical engineers in the United States and Canada, although many international clinical engineers have also been certified by the HTCC. Qualifications required to take the certification exam include 4 years of engineering experience (with 3 in CE) and a BS in engineering.

Professional Societies

The ACCE is the only professional society for clinical engineers in the United States. The AAMI is a well-known trade organization that serves the CE and healthcare technology management community, but it has a wide variety of areas of interest, including medical product manufacturing, central sterile process, and technology in nursing. There are many national and international BME professional organizations, but few that focus on CE. The International Federation of Medical and Biological Engineering (IFMBE) has a Clinical Engineering Division (CED) which focuses on the professional needs of the clinical engineering community. ACCE and AAMI would be good resources for any individual seeking a career in CE.

CAREER ADVANCEMENT

The primary way any individual can advance in his or her career is by working hard, being honest, and working for the success of his or her boss and organization. Accepting assignments and doing the best you can is always a good way to be of value. Individuals who try to improve themselves and take the long view of their career also do well. One way to improve yourself and advance your career is to always look for opportunities for professional improvement. This means improving yourself professionally. By taking a class or course offered by your employer, you will improve. By seeking outside training and attending professional meetings, you will improve your knowledge base. An excellent way to advance your career is by becoming certified. This can be a technical certification such as computer networking or a professional certification such as CCE. Doing this will show that you are interested in improving and willing to work to accomplish it, rather than coasting through life.

Another way to advance your career is to change jobs. If you are doing well with your current employer and the employer appreciates your services, then imagine how much more your employer would appreciate you if you knew firsthand how things work in another organization. True, many people would rather not move to gain a different set of experiences, but that would put them on a linear trajectory, which will slowly increase their salary and experience, with occasional bumps for promotions. If, however, you make a strategic job change to increase your salary and expand your experience, you will accelerate this upward trajectory. If stability is what you are looking for, you will do well in CE. Healthcare and technology will always be here. If you are looking to maximize the possibilities though, then change jobs a couple of times after 3–4 years of experience at each. The extra information and perspective and the professional value it will bring you will be worth the trouble.

Along the same vein, if you change jobs to learn about another area of CE, you will broaden your technical horizons. This will also increase your future value as an employee.

Perhaps you will get in a rut in your career, not feeling like you are advancing, even feeling like you are being taken advantage of. It is at this point a job change may do you the most good professionally. If you live in a major metropolitan area, this may be a fairly simple process, which may not even involve a move. Just remember, you can only do this once or twice and maybe even three times in your 40+-year career. Beyond that, you will get a negative reputation as a job hopper, which would not be good for your career advancement.

Another concept to consider is that the more management and supervisory responsibilities you take on, the faster your career will grow.

Career Ladders

An organization that advertises a career ladder and demonstrates how you can advance your career with it is generally a good organization to work for. A career ladder, that is, moving from one job to another, increasing your salary, and responsibilities, is a great way to advance your career. Most organizations say they have a career ladder, but they really have not given much thought to the human nature of wanting to advance and do more in our careers. It is up to you to evaluate what they have. A typical career ladder for a clinical engineer would be an advancement progression from clinical engineer to senior clinical engineer to CE supervisor to director of CE. If you have a young person doing well above you, hopefully you will both be promoted in synchronization. If you get too impatient, changing jobs for the promotion could be a solution.

COMPENSATION

Starting salaries vary by business cycle, geographical region, and the candidate's ability to impress, but generally, clinical engineers with a BS degree get a starting salary in the high-50s to mid-60s. Clinical engineers with an MS degree get a starting salary in the 70s. Most can expect to receive an annual salary increase in the 2%–6% range. This of course depends on the rate of inflation that year. Salary increases also come in the form of promotional raises, annual cost of living raises, performances raises, and periodic bonuses. The type of organization will dictate the form of the increase, but a well-performing and professional individual can expect to receive a raise every year that well exceeds the inflation index. Clinical engineers in management positions with a solid work history can reasonably achieve a salary of $120,000–150,000 or higher per year.

FREELANCE OPPORTUNITIES

Most clinical engineers can expect to be pretty busy with their regular job. Most will work 45–50h per week; some might work even more than that. Freelance or consulting opportunities are available with a little effort after you have some experience under your belt. If you are inclined to do work on the side, then think of the services you could offer that most CE departments do not have. Then contact department heads you may know outside your immediate area and offer your assistance. A successful career as part-time freelance consultant depends on good contacts and being responsive when you do get an engagement.

References

AAMI Future Forum III Article, www.aami.org/productspublications/articledetail.aspx? ItemNumber=1016.
ACCE Definitions, www.accenet.org.
Graduate Clinical Engineering Education, www.bme.uconn.edu.

CHAPTER FIVE

Cybersecurity

Angelique Dawkins
Baylor Scott & White Health, Dallas, Texas, United States

One of the most important issues impacting medical devices today is security. Most, if not all, healthcare professionals would agree that medical devices have changed rapidly in the recent years. It was not long ago that these devices were made almost entirely of hardware components. Today, however, the backbone of these devices is increasingly software driven. Many are running on operating systems we are all familiar with, such as Windows and Linux, and they are more interconnected than ever before. It is now common for devices to talk to each other over a network, send data directly to electronic medical records, and be remotely accessible via an Internet connection.

With medical devices having transformed so quickly, it is not surprising that the field of biomedical engineering has changed as well. Biomedical engineering professionals who work with medical devices have had to cultivate new skills to manage this equipment. Knowledge of information technology (IT) has become an integral part of this process. In order to understand how medical devices work, being well versed in computer hardware, software, and networking is essential, and just as important is knowing how to protect these devices from online threats.

This is where the field of cybersecurity comes in. Simply put, cybersecurity is the means by which devices, networks, and data are protected from unauthorized access and attack. Keeping networks and sensitive information safe has long been a concern for many organizations. But recent events have highlighted the need for better security measures, especially for medical devices and patient care environments. Of note, are cyberattacks such as WannaCry, a ransomware that spanned across the Internet in 2017. This ransomware operates by locking down and encrypting affected systems, denying access until a ransom is paid. Several healthcare systems were hit by this attack, resulting in disrupted operations and patient care. Unfortunately, the number of attacks such as WannaCry are only expected to increase over time. Medical devices can be vulnerable to these attacks if

Careers in Biomedical Engineering
ISBN 978-0-12-814816-7
https://doi.org/10.1016/B978-0-12-814816-7.00005-4

not secured, making cybersecurity knowledge a must-have for healthcare IT professionals.

A healthcare cybersecurity career can take many forms, as security is an issue throughout a device's life cycle. During manufacturing, security controls can be designed into the device before it hits the market, and ongoing patch development can continue after the device is in production. Once purchased by a healthcare delivery organization, they will want to make sure the device is secure on their network to safeguard patients and their health data. All of this is governed by the medical device and security standards developed by government and nonprofit organizations. As a cybersecurity professional, it is possible to make a career supporting any one of these endeavors.

MEDICAL DEVICE CYBERSECURITY CAREER PATHS

You will find that professionals in the medical device security field come from a variety of educational and training backgrounds. Some are current or former clinicians who have delved into the world of IT. Others may have started out in a more technical role, with formal education in engineering and science. There are still others who may have started out with completely unrelated backgrounds but have emerged as cybersecurity leaders. All this is to say that there are many routes you can take to break into this career field. Ultimately, medical device security is such a complex issue that biomedical engineering, IT, and security management are all valid paths.

Biomedical Engineering

Biomedical engineering professionals can be found impacting cybersecurity from all over the healthcare industry. Typical roles can include managing medical device inventory, research and development (R&D), and work on device standards. Managing an equipment inventory comes into play when working for healthcare systems, which includes hospitals and clinics. The biomedical engineering profession at these organizations is known as healthcare technology management (HTM), and is made up of biomedical engineers and biomedical engineering technicians (BMETs). The HTM staff are the medical device experts and keepers of a healthcare system's medical equipment inventory. They are the most familiar with these devices and their repair and maintenance history. BMETs are typically frontline staff that repair equipment, whereas biomedical engineers usually serve in a management or program support role.

HTM staff are a key part of any healthcare organization's approach to cybersecurity. They are among the first employees consulted when a device is suspected or confirmed to be compromised on the network. They are also some of the first to be notified by manufacturers of device recalls, which includes cybersecurity issues. In these instances, HTM staff would be directly involved in investigation and remediation efforts. They would be expected to either directly patch or work with the medical device manufacturer to patch compromised or vulnerable equipment. They would be expected to routinely update software on medical devices as those updates become available.

From an inventory management perspective, HTM staff should be tracking networking information for all their connected medical devices. While all HTM departments have a medical equipment database of what they maintain, the information tracked can vary from organization to organization. Cybersecurity-focused HTM departments will include information such as the operating system, antivirus, applied patches, Internet Protocol (IP) address, personal health information (PHI) storage capabilities, and other applicable network information for each device. This will be helpful for both troubleshooting device connectivity problems and remediation efforts during security incidents. Also, as HTM staff will be familiar with this information, they can advise clinical personnel of potential cybersecurity risks during medical device purchases. If there are concerns or issues that HTM staff believes the manufacturer should address, a resolution can be weaved into the purchasing or device rollout process. Ultimately, it is the job of HTM staff to keep abreast of emerging cybersecurity threats to medical devices and assist in the management of a robust security program.

For medical device manufacturers, possible roles in which biomedical engineers can work include R&D, regulatory compliance, and technical support. As an R&D engineer, responsibilities generally include device design activities such as creating and modifying device designs, developing testing protocols, monitoring engineering tests, troubleshooting when issues arise, and ensuring compliance with regulatory standards. Engineers taking cybersecurity into account would weave that into the design process. This should include programming in robust security controls and extensive testing to weed out potential vulnerabilities.

Some biomedical engineers choose to specialize entirely in regulatory compliance and are well-versed in laws and government regulations concerning medical devices. This includes guidance on the device approval process with the Food and Drug Administration (FDA), but ideally it should also include guidance concerning device cybersecurity. Regulatory compliance engineers would be a resource to the manufacturer during the device's design and testing phase, and after the device is released into the marketplace (known as a postmarket device).

In a technical support role, engineers respond to customer inquiries, which can include securing their medical devices against vulnerabilities or emerging malware threats. BMETs also have a role here, as many device manufacturers employ them as field support to repair devices for healthcare customers. In this capacity, they would be expected to install software updates and patches either on site or remotely (depending on the device configuration). This can occur in the case of a cybersecurity incident or manufacturer-driven remediation of a known vulnerability.

Biomedical engineers can also be employed by government agencies. One of these is FDA, in particular their Center for Devices and Radiological Health. Typical roles would include approving medical devices for manufacturers to sell, the monitoring of device recall actions, device incident investigations, and the creation of medical device policies and regulations. Cybersecurity comes into play with most of these job duties. For recalls, many are software issues needing correction by the manufacturer, which include patching for security vulnerabilities. FDA staff who monitor recall actions perform compliance checks to ensure that the manufacturer has attempted remediation with affected customers. As far as policies and regulations, the FDA engineers can also help with creating and revising cybersecurity standards. The FDA has recently begun releasing cybersecurity guidance to the field, focusing on security controls for premarket devices, patching devices after entering market, and management of devices on healthcare networks.

Security Analysts and Engineers

Similar to biomedical engineering professionals, security analysts and engineers (these terms are somewhat interchangeable) are on the front lines when it comes to securing systems from attacks. However, they protect devices from a different standpoint. They are experts at both finding vulnerabilities and building up defenses in devices and networks, making it one of the most valuable roles for any security-conscious organization. It is also one of the most technical career paths for those interested in medical device cybersecurity. To become a successful security analyst, you should have a firm grasp of networking and hacking concepts.

While many people associate hacking with criminal activity, the truth is that hackers play an important role in defending critical systems and infrastructure. They are often hired by governments and corporations to find weaknesses in their systems, or to help investigate security incidents. They are able to do this with a firm grasp of operating systems, networking concepts, programming, and security vulnerabilities. This level of expertise can also be applied to several aspects of medical device design and management.

Penetration testing is one of the essential tools analysts use to discover vulnerabilities. This requires simulating attacks on devices and trying to break down their security barriers. By performing these tests, they can identify exploitable vulnerabilities in a device or the network on which it resides. This can be done with the device in hand or by using a network to gain access. The ability to perform penetration tests is a highly sought-after skill for many organizations within the healthcare industry, including device manufactures, healthcare organizations, government agencies, and consulting firms. This gives security analysts interested in medical devices a great amount of flexibility in choosing a career path.

When working for manufacturers, their job is to ensure the security of product lines both before and after devices hit the market. They can be directly involved in product development, making sure the device complies with the latest security standards. They may also be involved in product testing, mapping out risk and attack scenarios, and correction of found vulnerabilities. As more manufacturers become interested in developing a standard security framework for their devices, analysts may be involved in that process as well. For devices that have already been released to the public, they can help with the development and testing of software revisions and patches. This may include assisting customers with applying these patches to their devices. They must also keep abreast of new threats that can impact the manufacturer's devices and be prepared to respond with mitigation strategies.

In healthcare delivery organizations, the role would be similar to that of working for a device manufacturer, but instead focused from the care provider's perspective. Healthcare organizations may want the security analyst to perform penetration testing on their devices and network. The organization could then make more informed decisions on how its devices should operate on the network, and improve its network security. This knowledge can also help the organization in future equipment purchasing decisions and in developing a potential list of security requirements that manufacturers should adhere to. Should the security analyst find vulnerabilities that are within a manufacturer's ability to fix, the healthcare organization can alert them to make improvements.

One other option for security analysts is a government role. For any country the security of its infrastructure is usually a top concern, which includes healthcare. As an analyst for the government, you may be tasked with compiling data on the latest cyber threats, investigating cybersecurity incidents, and assisting with remediation efforts. One agency that does all three of these activities is the National Cybersecurity and Communications Integration Center (NCCIC), a part of the Department of Homeland Security (DHS). NCCIC is composed of response teams that are sent out to organizations impacted by security incidents. These include the US Computer Emergency Readiness Team (US-CERT) and the Industrial Control Systems Cyber Emergency Response Team (ICS-CERT) (CERT). ICS-CERT specializes in critical infrastructure, whereas the mission of US-CERT is broader.

Other Information Technology Careers

Following are some common IT job titles for professionals involved with medical device security. It is by no means an exhaustive list, and specific job titles and duties will vary among organizations.

- Information security officer (ISO)/chief information security officer (CISO)
- Network engineer or architect
- Network operations specialist
- Technical support specialist

Positions such as the network engineer (or network architect) and operations specialist focus on maintaining the healthcare network. These professionals know how to design, implement, and troubleshoot various networking solutions. This can include deploying and monitoring servers, switches, routers, and other networking equipment. As this equipment is often used to support the operation of medical devices, the HTM staff will collaborate with IT specialists during network-caused device outages. These IT roles may also assist in implementing security measures on the network.

ISOs are IT professionals specializing in security and risk management. They are responsible for managing all aspects of security programs at the organizations they serve. ISOs may also be referred to as CISOs at organizations where they oversee network security personnel. The CISO is usually an executive-level position with a high level of visibility. Job duties for an ISO or a CISO may include

- developing a security program that adheres to the law and industry practices,
- performing risk assessments and identifying at-risk devices or network segments,
- writing corporate security policies,
- communicating the organization's security strategy to key stakeholders,
- hiring and managing IT personnel,
- providing cybersecurity expertise for IT projects,
- investigating, or managing the investigation of, security incidents.

Biomedical Engineering and Information Technology: Working Together

In healthcare delivery organizations, HTM and IT staff come together to support device security efforts. Threats to medical devices here are typically twofold. First, viruses or other malware can infect a medical device and affect its operation (coming either from removable media or from Internet access). Second, by exploiting vulnerabilities in medical device software, someone can gain access to the hospital network and patient information or even affect the operation of the device. It is the responsibility of HTM and IT staff to prevent these situations, or mitigate them if they do occur.

Personnel on the information security or IT side will usually hold the keys to the healthcare network. IT staff should be able to monitor network traffic to and from these devices and perform vulnerability scans. If the scans detect viruses or malware, they can shut down ports or wireless access to the affected device. Also they would be responsible for increasing security to prevent intrusions on the clinical network. Meanwhile, HTM staff will have direct access to devices and be the most familiar with their operation. They should bring IT staff and the device manufacturer together to ensure devices are secure on the network. This includes determining whether antivirus can be installed on devices and if security scans will impact device operation. If antivirus and scans can take place, HTM staff will need to facilitate discussion between IT staff and the manufacturer on how this can be implemented. For devices where this is not possible, the discussion should move to protecting them using the organization's own network. This can include segmenting devices from one another or the use of firewalls, among other solutions.

There are several unique challenges that HTM and IT staff face in this environment. One, cybersecurity as a major concern for medical devices is still a relatively new concept in healthcare. Only in the last few years has it come into focus as a major issue. Therefore many healthcare systems are just beginning to develop a framework in which their devices are routinely monitored and patched. This is complicated by the fact that many devices that are running on old and outdated software, with few security controls. Another challenge is that security has to revolve around patient care. Medical devices are integral to clinical operations, which means that often equipment is in use. This can leave very little downtime to perform routine maintenance or urgent patching. HTM and IT staff must often work together to secure devices with as little disruption as possible.

SALARY AND CAREER OUTLOOK

The career outlook for cybersecurity jobs is excellent, and should be for years to come. This is due to many organizations, especially in healthcare, being new to the concept of cyber defense. In a 2017 survey of security leaders from companies worldwide, 44% stated they do not have an information security strategy, whereas 54% admitted they do not have a cybersecurity incident response process (Casteli et al., 2017). With the rise in cyberattacks each year, it is clear they need employees who are well versed in cybersecurity concepts. Unfortunately, for these organizations, there are many cybersecurity jobs open but not enough qualified people to fill them.

According to the International Information System Security Certification Consortium $(ISC)^2$, an international nonprofit dedicated to network security, 1.8 million more cybersecurity professionals are needed to close the workforce gap by 2022 (McGraw Hill Cybersecurity Infographic). For security analysts alone, in 2016, there were 112,000 openings in the United States and approximately 96,870 workers filling them. The average time it took a corporation to find qualified professionals for those jobs was 96 days (CyberSeek Supply/Demand Heat Map). As you can see, there are plenty of opportunities available for those interested in a cybersecurity career. Also salaries for these positions can be quite high. In 2016 the average salary for a security analyst was $92,600 (US Bureau of Labor Statistics). For those in an ISO role the salary is even higher, with a median income of $214,804 (Chief Information Security Officer Salaries).

EDUCATION AND TRAINING

Now that you have an idea of career possibilities in the field, it is time to ask yourself where your interests lie. Some things you might want to ask yourself include the following:

Do you like the idea of working in a hospital environment? If so are you more interested in working directly with medical devices or in an IT support role?

Do you enjoy software programming?

Does the idea of R&D of medical devices excite you?

Are you interested in the development of standards for medical devices? How about performing compliance checks with medical device manufacturers?

Once you have decided which of these paths most appeal to you, it is time to consider what kind of education and technical skills will be the most helpful. Given the flexibility of this career choice, you can start out in one path and end up in another. The following majors might be appealing:

Biomedical engineering and biomedical engineering technology

Majoring in biomedical engineering or biomedical engineering technology is a good choice if you are looking to work directly with medical equipment. However, many universities may not offer classes specific to medical device security. If that is the case for a program of interest, instead consider supplementing with courses that cover programming, networking, security, or other computer science topics. In fact, a minor in computer science or similar field is a good idea.

Computer science or computer engineering

Computer science or engineering may be a good choice for those interested in becoming a security analyst or in developing and managing medical device software for manufacturers. Some universities even offer concentrations that are cybersecurity focused. Both the majors should give you a solid foundation in computer architecture and programming.

Information systems or IT

You are most likely familiar with IT as a major that will advance your skills with computers and networking. This path is a good one if your interests lie in maintaining and troubleshooting networks. Some schools will offer additional courses pertinent to cybersecurity, or even an IT degree with a focus on cybersecurity.

Cybersecurity

A growing number of institutions are beginning to offer undergraduate and graduate programs in cybersecurity. Some also offer graduate certificates, which are shorter programs offering less courses, and not leading to a degree. For graduate programs or certificates, there are some institutions that focus the curriculum more toward the working professional, meaning nighttime or online course offerings.

It is important to research the coursework and concentrations offered at universities that interest you, as there is some variability in the programs offered. Some university programs are in schools of business, computer science, engineering, or a combination of these and others. Concentrations and focused coursework you may find include:

- digital forensics
- networking and security
- information assurance
- risk management
- laws and regulations

Schools to Consider

The Association for the Advancement of Medical Instrumentation (AAMI) has compiled a comprehensive list of biomedical engineering and BMET programs throughout the United States. You can find this listing on their Professional Development page: http://www.aami.org/professionaldevelopment/content.aspx?ItemNumber=1219&navItemNumber=1311.

There is also a database of schools available for those wanting to pursue a strictly cybersecurity-based curriculum. The DHS and the National Security Administration (NSA) have partnered to sponsor two cybersecurity programs. These are the National Centers of Academic Excellence in Cyber Defense (CAE-CD) program and the National Centers of Academic Excellence in Cyber Operations (CAE-Cyber Operations) program. These programs provide guidelines to educational institutions offering cybersecurity degrees. For a degree program to receive recognition, it must meet specific criteria. These include "knowledge units," which are courses that cover mandatory (and some optional) topics set by the DHS and NSA (National Centers of Academic Excellence in Cyber Defense).

Once an institution meets the CAE-CD criteria, it becomes recognized by these two federal agencies. Under this program, an institution can be designated as a center of excellence in cyber defense education (CAE-CDE), 2-year education (CAE-2Y), or research (CAE-R).

Meanwhile, the CAE-Cyber Operations program is sponsored solely by the NSA and is designed as a complement to the Cyber Defense program. Institutions that meet the CAE-Cyber Operations criteria offer degree programs that are highly technical and give hands-on experience, such as computer science, computer engineering, or electrical engineering (National Centers of Academic Excellence in Cyber Defense). The list of institutions recognized as National Centers of Academic Excellence is accessible online at nsa.gov. These include colleges, universities, or technical schools.

Some schools designated as CAE-DE or CAE-Cyber Operations may also take part in the CyberCorps: Scholarships for Service program. This scholarship program is funded by the National Science Foundation and may partially or fully fund your cybersecurity-related degree program. In order to qualify, you must agree to work in public service after graduation. This means working for the federal government in a cybersecurity role for a duration equal to the length of the scholarship (CyberCorp Scholarships for Service). This is an excellent opportunity for those looking to break into a cybersecurity role early in their career.

It should be noted that it is possible to cross-refer the list of schools offering cybersecurity degrees with AAMI's list of biomedical engineering programs. This might prove useful for anyone not only wanting to major in biomedical engineering or biomedical engineering technology but also wanting to take cybersecurity courses. Conversely, this would be helpful for anyone wanting to major in IT field but wishing to have some exposure to biomedical engineering coursework.

Internships

Completing internships while in school is one of the best ways to kick-start your career after graduation. Internships provide you with valuable experience that can go on your resume, and expand your network of professional contacts. Keep in mind that where you complete your internships can help shape your career. For exposure to the healthcare industry, it would be worthwhile to intern at a medical device manufacturer or healthcare system. Besides options in private industry, the US government also offers some good security-focused programs. However, while government internships are good for developing valuable cybersecurity experience, they are unlikely to focus specifically on medical devices. One such internship program is the Cyber Student Volunteer Initiative (CSVI). The CSVI is a 10-week internship program sponsored by the DHS. Interns are given the opportunity to work alongside cybersecurity professionals and gain skills through hands-on assignments. Departments that the intern can be assigned to can vary and positions can be open nationwide (Cybersecurity Volunteer Initiative).

Other Training Opportunities

There are plenty of resources available besides a college degree for learning about IT and cybersecurity. Online, self-paced learning and in-person training programs are both excellent choices. In order to find courses that are right for you consider looking on the National Initiative for Cybersecurity Career and Studies (NICCS) website. NICCS is a part of the DHS and is dedicated to providing educational resources to those seeking a cybersecurity career. Anyone can use their search feature to look up training classes offered around the United States. Training classes are provided by a number of different companies, and may be online or in person. The NICCS training search engine is https://niccs.us-cert.gov/training/search.

In addition to NICCS, there are several websites offering free online IT and cybersecurity training. These include

- Cybrary.it
- Coursera
- edX
- Codecademy
- Microsoft Virtual Academy
- OpenSecurityTraining.info

Cybrary.it and OpenSecurityTraining.info specifically address IT and security topics. Codecademy and Microsoft Virtual Academy are aimed at those learning to program. Coursera and edX are among several platforms hosting free courses on a variety of subjects, and networking or security courses may be among those offered.

Training for Veterans and US Government Employees

NICCS has set up a training portal specifically for veterans and government employees. This portal is the Federal Virtual Training Environment (FedVTE). FedVTE is free and has an extensive catalog of courses. These courses include, but are not limited to, certification preparation, programming, cybersecurity risk management, networking, and penetration testing. The full list of cybersecurity training can be found on the NICCS website: https://niccs.us-cert.gov/training/federal-virtual-training-environment-fedvte.

KNOWLEDGE, SKILLS, AND ABILITIES

You may be wondering what basic skills you need in order to succeed in a cybersecurity role. Fortunately, there is a resource available to job seekers that maps out the basic knowledge, skills, and abilities (known as KSAs) needed for these positions. The National Institute of Standards and Technology (NIST) has partnered with other government agencies and private-sector corporations to form the National Initiative for Cybersecurity Education (NICE). The goal of NICE is to promote a network of cybersecurity education and training resources for job seekers, corporations, and educational institutions. One of the resources they have developed is the NICE Cybersecurity Workforce Framework, which lists out the basic competencies for the many career paths available in this field. This framework applies to IT as a whole and is not specific to the healthcare industry.

There are seven total categories that jobs in this framework can be grouped under:
- Securely provision
- Operate and maintain
- Oversee and govern
- Protect and defend
- Analyze
- Collect and operate
- Investigate

Each category is made up of several specialty areas. For example, under the protect and defend category, some of the specialty areas include cyber defense analysis, incident response, and vulnerability assessment and management. Each category and specialty area is clearly defined by the framework.

Let us take a look at the security analyst role described earlier in the chapter. Based on this framework, a security analyst can actually be several jobs depending on your area of specialization. It differentiates between analysts with expertise in vulnerability assessment and analysts who respond to cyber incidents. However, there are some commonalities among analyst job descriptions. An analyst should have knowledge of (Newhouse et al., 2017)
- computer networking and protocols (such as Transmission Control Protocol and IP, Open System Interconnection Model, and IT Infrastructure Library);
- operating systems;
- network security principles (such as firewalls, demilitarized zones, etc.), models, and architecture (topology, protocols, components, etc.);

- security models (such as the Bell–LaPadula model, Biba integrity model, Clark–Wilson integrity model);
- network access and identity management (e.g., public key infrastructure, OAuth, OpenID, Security Assertion Markup Language, Security Provisioning Markup Language);
- risk management, including policies and procedures;
- cyber threats and vulnerabilities, including the ability to recognize them, how to conduct vulnerability scans, and using networking tools to identify them;
- cryptography;
- encryption algorithms;
- vulnerability information sources (such as advisories and bulletins);
- PHI and personally identifiable information security standards;
- user credential management.

Biomedical engineering professionals interested in cybersecurity should also have a firm grasp of the abovementioned concepts. These are essential for truly understanding how medical devices operate on a network and how to protect these devices from cyberattacks.

For more information on the framework and additional job descriptions check out the NICE homepage: https://www.nist.gov/itl/applied-cybersecurity/nice.

CERTIFICATIONS

One of the most important avenues to achieve success in this field is gaining and maintaining certifications. In particular, IT- and security-related certifications will show mastery of networking and security concepts and can help qualify you for more advanced jobs. In fact, close to 70% of organizations require certifications for open security positions (State of Cyber Security, 2017). Following are some of the most common certifications held by medical device security experts. Although many of these are for more advanced security professionals, there are several that can be taken by those early in their career.

Computing Technology Industry Association Certifications

For those starting out in their career or beginning their immersion in the world of IT and security, you may want to consider Computing Technology Industry Association (CompTIA) certifications. The certifications that the CompTIA provides are vendor neutral and will test you on the fundamentals of computers, networking, and security.

A+

The A+ certification covers the basics of PCs and mobile devices, with a focus on troubleshooting and repairing hardware and software. This is a good certification for those who have a background in technical support. Although there is no required level of work experience needed, it is recommended that exam takers have a few months of hands-on experience.

Network+

The Network+ certification covers the basics of managing and troubleshooting both wired and wireless networks. The recommended amount of networking experience needed before taking this exam is 9 months; however, there is no requirement.

Security+

The Security+ certification covers the basics of securing systems and devices, risk assessment, and identifying and mitigating cyber threats and vulnerabilities. There is no requirement for taking this exam; however, it is recommended to have the Network+ certification first, or several years of relevant work experience.

CySA+ (CyberSecurity Analyst)

The CySA+ is a newer certification offered by CompTIA. It is designed for those who have the Network+ and Security+ certifications, or who have at least 3–4 years of relevant work experience. Takers of this exam should have the ability to use threat detection tools, to identify vulnerabilities, and to properly secure devices and systems on a network.

CompTIA Advanced Security Practitioner

The CompTIA Advanced Security Practitioner (CASP) is the most advanced cybersecurity certification offered by CompTIA. This certification is recommended for professionals with approximately 5 years of experience (CompTIA Certifications).

Cisco Certifications

While geared toward networking with Cisco products, these certifications are recognized throughout the industry and are held by many IT professionals. Cisco certification levels can range from beginner to advanced for security practitioners. Beginner certifications include the Cisco Certified Entry Networking Technician (CCENT) and Cisco Certified Technician

(CCT). Cisco's other certifications are classified as Cisco Certified Network Associate (CCNA), Cisco Certified Network Professional (CCNP), or Cisco Certified Internetwork Expert (CCIE). Associate indicates a certification appropriate for those early in their career. Professional is targeted for those mid-career, while Expert indicates an advanced certification.

Certifications for network and security topics are offered for all career levels. Network-focused certifications include, but are not limited to, Routing and Switching, Wireless, and Cloud. There are two security-focused certifications: Security and Cyber Ops. While Security is offered for all career levels, Cyber Ops is only offered at the Associate level (Cisco Training and Certifications).

(ISC)² Certifications

$(ISC)^2$ is an international nonprofit association for network security, and it offers certifications for IT professionals. These certifications are generally for those having some years of work experience. The most common are listed in the following from least to most advanced.

Systems Security Certified Practitioner

This security certification requires at least 1 year of work experience in a qualifying area. However, work experience can be waived for those who have a degree in cybersecurity.

Certified Secure Software Lifecycle Professional

This certification is designed for those involved in the security of software applications during development. This can be at the development, testing, or management level. At least 4 years of work experience is required to take the certification exam.

Certified Information Systems Security Professional

The Certified Information Systems Security Professional (CISSP) is a cybersecurity certification that requires at least 5 years of work experience in the field and is considered an advanced certification. There are several certifications under the CISSP umbrella, including CISSP, CISSP-ISSAP (Information Systems Security Architecture Professional), CISSP-ISSEP (Information Systems Security Engineering Professional), and CISSP-ISSMP (Information Systems Security Management Professional). CISSP is the base certification, which you must receive before testing for the additional ISSAP, ISSEP, or ISSMP designations ((ISC)^2 Information Security Certifications).

Information Systems Audit and Control Association Certifications

The Information Systems Audit and Control Association is a nonprofit organization that develops Information Systems standards and educational content. It offers IT certifications designed to show proficiency in several aspects of organizational IT management, including auditing, enterprise system management, and risk management. These certifications are geared toward those who are more advanced in their career, and each requires at least several years of work experience. Listed in the following are a few of its security-focused certifications.

Certified Information Security Manager

The CISM certification is for those experienced in organizational security management. The exam covers information security governance, risk management, security program development, and security incident management. Recommended takers of this exam should have at least 5 years of experience.

Certified Information Systems Auditor

The CISA certification is geared toward professionals involved in information security auditing or security. The exam covers auditing information systems, IT governance, information systems acquisition and maintenance, and asset protection. At least 5 years of experience is required before taking the exam.

Certified in Risk and Information Systems Control

The CRISC certification gauges proficiency in IT risk management, covering risk identification, assessment, monitoring, mitigation, and reporting. At least 3 years of experience is required to take this exam (ISACA Certification).

Global Information Assurance Certification Certifications

Global Information Assurance Certification (GIAC) is a program offering certifications for IT professionals, ranging from entry- to advanced-level of expertise. All certifications offered by GIAC are topic specific and are valid for 4 years. The categories of their certifications include (GIAC Certifications Get Certified Roadmap) the following:

- Cyber defense
- Penetration testing
- Digital forensics and incident response
- Developer
- Management & leadership
- Security expert

CONFERENCES

Attending conferences is a great way to learn about new issues affecting the industry, receive continuing education, and network with experts and peers. There are several conferences you may want to consider attending if you are in the biomedical engineering field and interested in cybersecurity topics.

Healthcare Information and Management Systems Society

Healthcare Information and Management Systems Society (HIMSS) is an international nonprofit organization dedicated to improve healthcare through IT. The organization offers many education and professional development opportunities, including newsletters, webinars, conferences, and online communities where healthcare IT professionals can discuss specific topics. The HIMSS organizations exist at the continent level, such as HIMSS North America, HIMSS Europe, and HIMSS Asia, as well as include local chapters. Many chapters will host regular in-person meetings, which is an excellent opportunity for networking and keeping abreast of the latest healthcare IT issues. HIMSS chapters also hold regional and national conferences. These are usually well attended not only by healthcare IT professionals but also by medical device manufacturers.

Association for the Advancement of Medical Instrumentation

AAMI is a nonprofit organization dedicated to healthcare technology. It provides many resources to the healthcare community, including continuing education, conferences, and standards development. AAMI holds a conference once per year that is well attended by device manufacturers and HTM professionals. It is an excellent opportunity to receive education on medical device issues and to network with peers.

Archimedes Center for Medical Device Security

The Archimedes Center for Medical Device Security is a US nonprofit dedicated to cybersecurity issues affecting the medical device industry. Members include device manufacturers, healthcare delivery organizations, and cybersecurity firms. Archimedes holds an annual conference that is attended by these and government organizations such as the FDA. Conference sessions focus on the latest cybersecurity threats affecting the industry and how healthcare organizations are managing their security programs.

Black Hat

Black Hat is a well-known conference where hackers and other information security professionals gather to hear the latest news in security research. Security researchers give briefings on vulnerabilities they have discovered, which can be applicable to any number of devices, systems, or industries. Black Hat is made up of several chapters by continent, including Black Hat USA, Europe, and Asia.

Security BSides

BSides groups exist all over the world and in many major cities and are localized organizations offering security conferences and training. While the groups themselves are rather informal, the topics covered at their events are in a similar vein to Black Hat. Specific topics will vary based on the local security experts available to speak, but will cover hacking and security issues.

SANS Institute

The SANS Institute is an organization that offers IT and security training to professionals all over the world. SANS Institute hosts several conferences a year, which are mass training events where attendees can pick from a large list of available IT and security courses. Many of these courses help fulfill requirements for certifications.

SECURITY ANALYST SKILL DEVELOPMENT

If you have decided to go the route of a security analyst or similar role, you should consider becoming involved in the hacking community. It is a good way to continue developing your skills and to see where you stack up against other hackers. Networking and job opportunities may also become available. Two common ways to become more involved is participation in competitions and bug bounty programs.

Competitions

Participating in competitions is an excellent way to test your knowledge of cybersecurity, and see how you stack up against others in the field. Depending on the nature of the competition, it can also be a good networking tool. Some competitions are in-person events, whereas others are strictly online. Resources for competitions include the US Cyber Challenge (USCC) program.

US Cyber Challenge

The USCC is a program sponsored by the DHS and the Center for Internet Security. It is designed to attract, train, and recruit individuals interested in cybersecurity, from high-school students to those who are already working professionals. The program sponsors cybersecurity-focused competitions and training camps.

Cyber Quest competitions hosted by USCC are online, and test participants on different aspects of cybersecurity. Difficulty can range from beginner to expert level. Those participating have their scores ranked, and the winner will have received the highest score in the shortest amount of time. Potential prizes can include awards, scholarships, or admission to one of USCC's training camps (CyberQuests).

USCC camps are 1-week-long experiences focusing on specialized cybersecurity training. There are several held each year in the United States, and they are open to US citizens only. Those who are admitted to a camp are invited after earning a spot via a Cyber Quest competition. Activities at the camp include workshops, a "Capture the Flag" competition, and a job fair (USCC Cyber Challenge Cyber Camps).

Another resource sponsored by USCC is CyberCompEx, an online community dedicated to cybersecurity. CyberCompEx contains a forum for discussing cybersecurity issues and training resources, and a list of online cybersecurity competitions. Competitions are listed according to where they fall within the NICE framework.

Bug Bounty Programs

Bug bounty programs are designed to be a two-way street between organizations and the hacking community. Organizations that need help finding vulnerabilities in their systems offer a cash reward (the bounty) in exchange for successful discoveries. Hackers who complete the task claim the reward and get bragging rights for their work.

The HackerOne website hosts a public directory of organizations offering bug bounty programs. It is also a sponsor of the Internet Bug Bounty (IBB) program. The IBB program offers bounties for hackers who find vulnerabilities in Internet infrastructure or open source code. For more information refer to their bug bounty page: https://hackerone.com/bug-bounty-programs (Internet Bug Bounty).

REGULATION AND STANDARDS

One of the largest roadblocks for the healthcare industry is the lack of a medical device security roadmap. Many organizations are just beginning to tackle the problem of how to secure their devices and the networks on which they reside. Device manufacturers must increasingly work security controls into their device designs and manage updates to their devices after entering market. In the midst of this, there are organizations tasked with developing medical device and cybersecurity regulations and guidance. This is an excellent opportunity for anyone interested in writing policies that can shape the industry.

The following are medical device and cybersecurity standards to be aware of.

FDA Guidance

The FDA has released several guidance documents concerning medical device cybersecurity. They cover risk management of device security both before and after a medical device is released into the marketplace. Recommendations within these documents are nonbinding, but they are valued throughout the healthcare industry. Some of the documents are listed in the following:

- Content of Premarket Submissions for Management of Cybersecurity in Medical Devices
- Postmarket Management of Cybersecurity in Medical Devices
- Guidance to Industry: Cybersecurity for Networked Medical Devices Containing Off-the-Shelf (OTS) Software (Cybersecurity, 2018)

These and other documents are publicly available and can be found on the FDA Digital Health page: https://www.fda.gov/MedicalDevices/DigitalHealth/default.htm. The website also includes reports, webinars, and safety communications regarding known vulnerabilities and remediation steps.

International Organization for Standardization/International Electrotechnical Commission Standards

The International Organization for Standardization has created standards for almost every existing industry and is well known across the globe. The International Electrotechnical Commission focuses on standards for electronic technologies. These two organizations have collaborated on several standards for cybersecurity and medical devices. These include:

- International Organization for Standardization/International Electrotechnical Commission (ISO/IEC) 27000

     The ISO/IEC 27000 family of standards covers managing a security program, including how to safeguard protected information, implement a security program based on risk management, conduct security audits, and evaluate the effectiveness of an organization's security program (ISO/IEC 27000).

- ISO/IEC 80001

     The ISO/IEC 80001 family of standards covers risk management for IT networks incorporating medical devices. It defines the organizational responsibilities and actions necessary to keep devices safe and secure on a healthcare network (IEC 80001–1:2010).

Health Insurance Portability and Accountability Act

The US Department of Health and Human Services was given the authority to write safeguards for electronic health information by the Health Insurance Portability and Accountability Act (HIPAA) of 1996. HIPAA encompasses two rules: the HIPAA Privacy Rule and the HIPAA Security Rule. The Privacy Rule mandates how personally identifiable health information be kept secure, while the Security rule extends that to include electronic records (HIPAA for Professionals, 2017). These requirements are strictly followed by healthcare providers.

AAMI Technical Information Report 57

Technical Information Report (TIR) 57 is a guidance document developed by AAMI, entitled the Principles for Medical Device Security—Risk Management. It is primarily aimed at medical device manufacturers and shows them how to implement the risk management program described in the ISO 14971 standard (AAMI TIR57:2016). ISO 14971 is also a manufacturer-oriented standard, describing how to identify potential device hazards.

Digital Imaging and Communications in Medicine and Health Level Seven International

Digital Imaging and Communications in Medicine (DICOM) and Health Level Seven International (HL7) are both protocols for the exchange of healthcare information between systems. DICOM is the standard for transmitting healthcare images. HL7 is a set of standards that allows for the exchange of nonimaging health data. These two standards allow devices from different manufacturers to talk to each other, computers, and other peripherals. This concept is known as interoperability.

ADDITIONAL RESOURCES

Finding a Job

NICE Cybersecurity Framework

The NICE Cybersecurity Framework was designed to be a comprehensive resource describing the various cybersecurity roles available, and outlining the KSAs necessary to succeed in these roles. The KSAs cover IT, management, and policy development roles, but do not cover biomedical engineering. This Cybersecurity Framework can be found on the NIST website: https://www.nist.gov/itl/applied-cybersecurity/nice/resources/nice-cybersecurity-workforce-framework.

Cyberseek

Cyberseek is an online platform designed to help job seekers interested in cybersecurity. It includes up-to-date information about cybersecurity jobs around the United States and outlines how to advance along some common career pathways in the industry. Information includes an interactive map of the United States showing cybersecurity job supply and demand (www.cyberseek.org).

Vulnerability Databases and Bulletins

US Computer Emergency Readiness Team

To keep abreast of the latest threats, you should consider regularly visiting the US-CERT bulletin database. The website lists weekly updates of threats and includes information on patching when available. These bulletins also include cybersecurity threats pertinent to medical devices: https://www.us-cert.gov/ncas/bulletins.

Exploit Database

The Exploit Database is a website containing a comprehensive list of known exploits and vulnerabilities. Anyone can submit an exploit for publication if it can be verified. The exploit code can be downloaded, and in some cases the affected application can be as well. The Exploit Database also hosts white papers and e-magazines that discuss topics relevant to hacking (https://www.exploit-db.com).

Device Security Management
OWASP Secure Medical Device Deployment Standard
OWASP is the Open Web Application Security Project, a nonprofit focused on software security. Their medical device guide addresses how to securely deploy devices in healthcare facilities. It covers a range of considerations, including security controls on the device itself, network infrastructure, user access, and how to implement incident response plans (OWASP, 2017). The standard can be found at https://www.owasp.org/index.php/OWASP_Secure_Medical_Device_Deployment_Standard.

Manufacturer Disclosure Statement for Medical Device Security
The Manufacturer Disclosure Statement for Medical Device Security (MDS2) is a form provided by HIMSS. It allows manufacturers to disclose the system and security requirements of their devices (MDS2). Security-conscious organizations should routinely collect an MDS2 for each unique model of equipment they purchase. The MDS2 can be downloaded from HIMSS at http://www.himss.org/resourcelibrary/MDS2.

References

AAMI TIR 57:2016, June 5, 2016. Principles for Medical Device Security-Risk Management. Available at: http://my.aami.org/aamiresources/previewfiles/TIR57_1607_Preview.pdf.

Casteli, C., Gabriel, B., Yates, J., Booth, P., 2017. Strengthening Digital Society against Cyber Shocks. Available at: https://www.pwc.com/us/en/cybersecurity/assets/pwc-2018-gsiss-strengthening-digital-society-against-cyber-shocks.pdf.

National Cybersecurity Communications Integration Center. Available at: https://www.us-cert.gov/nccic.

Chief Information Security Officer Salaries. Available at: https://www1.salary.com/Chief-Information-Security-Officer-Salary.html.

Cisco Training and Certifications. Available at: https://www.cisco.com/c/en/us/training-events/training-certifications/certifications.html.

CompTIA Certifications. Available at: https://certification.comptia.org/certifications.

CyberCorp Scholarships for Service. Available at: https://www.sfs.opm.gov.

CyberQuests. Available at: https://uscc.cyberquests.org/.

Cybersecurity, February 7, 2018. Available at: https://www.fda.gov/MedicalDevices/DigitalHealth/ucm373213.htm.

Cybersecurity Volunteer Initiative. Available at: https://www.dhs.gov/homeland-security-careers/cyber-student-volunteer-initiative.

CyberSeek Supply/Demand Heat Map. Available at: http://cyberseek.org/heatmap.html.

GIAC Certifications Get Certified Roadmap. Available at: https://www.giac.org/certi
fications/get-certified/roadmap.

HIPAA for Professionals, June 16, 2017. Available at: https://www.hhs.gov/hipaa/for-
professionals/index.html.

IEC 80001–1:2010 Application of risk management for IT-networks incorporation medical
devices. Available at: https://www.iso.org/standard/44863.html.

Internet Bug Bounty. Available at: https://internetbugbounty.org.

ISACA Certification: IT Audit, Security, Governance, and Risk. Available at: http://www.
isaca.org/CERTIFICATION/Pages/default.aspx.

(ISC)2 Information Security Certifications. Available at: https://www.isc2.org/Certifications.

ISO/IEC 27000 family – Information security management systems. Available at: https://
www.iso.org/isoiec-27001-information-security.html.

McGraw Hill Cybersecurity Infographic. Available at: https://learn.mheducation.com/
2017--18-CompTIA-Infographic-CyberSecurity_2018-CompTIA-CS-Blog-LP.
html?&utm_source=cybersec-blogpromo&utm_campaign=2018-security-
plus09&utm_medium=referral&utm_content=comptia-info.

Manufacturer Disclosure Statement for Medical Device Security (MDS2). Available at:
http://www.himss.org/resourcelibrary/MDS2.

National Centers of Academic Excellence in Cyber Defense. (May 3, 2016). Available at:
https://www.nsa.gov/resources/educators/centers-academic-excellence/cyber-defense/.

Newhouse, W., Keith, S., Scribner, B., Witte, G., August 2017. National Initiative for
Cybersecurity Education (NICE) Cybersecurity Workforce Framework. Available at:
http://nvlpubs.nist.gov/nistpubs/SpecialPublications/NIST.SP.800-181.pdf.

OWASP Secure Medical Device Deployment Standard, March 20, 2017. Available at: https://
www.owasp.org/index.php/OWASP_Secure_Medical_Device_Deployment_Standard.

State of Cyber Security 2017 Part 1: Current Trends in Workforce Development, 2017.
Available at: http://www.isaca.org/Knowledge-Center/Research/Documents/state-
of-cybersecurity-2017_res_eng_0217.pdf?regnum=428485.

US Bureau of Labor Statistics: Occupational Outlook Handbook: Information Security
Analyst. Available at: https://www.bls.gov/ooh/computer-and-information-technol-
ogy/information-security-analysts.htm.

USCC Cyber Challenge Cyber Camps. Available at: https://www.uscyberchallenge.org/
cyber-camps/.

CHAPTER SIX

Freelance Opportunities

David Braeutigam[1,2]
[1]Brautigan Enterprises LLC, Arlington, TX, United States; [2]Healthcare Management Consultant, Arlington, TX, United States

A clinical engineer or biomedical equipment technician typically works for a hospital, a manufacturer (GE, Philips, Siemens, Abbott, etc.), or a third-party service company or vendor (GE, Philips, Aramark, Sodexo, Crothall, Modern Biomedical & Imaging, etc.) in healthcare technology management (HTM).

Their jobs within these organizations can include preventive maintenance inspections and repair of medical equipment, managing recalls, serving on hospital committees, advising on equipment selection, medical equipment security, medical equipment installation, and managing a HTM department.

There are numerous opportunities to work outside these companies if you desire. These opportunities include

- performing part-time freelance work while you still work full time in a hospital,
- working full time on a freelance basis with one company,
- working full time as a consultant, or
- Working full time as a one-person company.

The freelance opportunities include these titles:

- consultant
- expert witness,
- medical equipment planner,
- rehabilitation engineer,
- forensic engineer.

A consultant may offer some or all these options when they work with hospitals and medical equipment vendors. If you decide to work as a consultant part time while still employed then be sure to contact your employer and fill out the necessary conflict of interest documents (Dyro, 2004).

There are also freelance writing opportunities, some of which may be compensated in some way, for magazines and for certain other publications.

Careers in Biomedical Engineering
ISBN 978-0-12-814816-7
https://doi.org/10.1016/B978-0-12-814816-7.00006-6

HEALTHCARE TECHNOLOGY MANAGEMENT CONSULTANT

One option is to work as an HTM consultant. A consultant is someone who offers expert advice or services to a customer. In healthcare, HTM consultants are employed considerably by hospitals and manufacturers to help solve issues their staff cannot solve or do not have the time to solve. Many times a client will seek the advice of a consultant to audit their HTM program to look for new and fresh opportunities (Dickey et al., 2003).

The consultant needs to be seen as an expert in his/her field by constantly writing articles, attending healthcare conferences, speaking at professional organizations, and even publishing books. You can also supplement this by using your LinkedIn profile and Twitter, blogging, and other social media communication tools to market your business. You should also join professional organizations to keep you current on the latest issues and trends that are in healthcare. Key organizations in this field include the Association for the Advancement of Medical Instrumentation (AAMI, 2018), the American College of Clinical Engineering (ACCE, 2018), the American College of Healthcare Executives (ACHE, 2018), the American Society for Healthcare Engineering (ASHE, 2018), the Healthcare Information and Management Systems Society (HIMSS, 2018), and the Institute of Management Consultants (IMC, 2018). All these organizations have annual conferences and publications and offer great networking opportunities. Writing articles in these publications or speaking at their annual conferences is a great way to get your name out there and obtain new clients and business.

Two great sources for the consulting business can be found by reading consulting books and listening to audio books. *Million Dollar Consulting* by Alan Weiss, PhD, is a highly rated book and walks you through the business of consulting. It is available on Amazon in print, in Kindle, and as an audio book. *The McKinsey Mind* by Ethan M. Rasiel and Paul N. Friga outlines their experience of working with the great consulting company McKinsey and shares the lessons they learned. It is also available in print, in Kindle, and as an audio book. *An Insider's Guide to Building a Successful Consulting Practice* by Bruce L. Katcher, PhD, is another recommended book. It is available in print and Kindle. Audio books are a great use of your time when you are flying or driving to see a client. Audible books is a great source for audio books. It is now owned by Amazon and thus is a great one-stop source to buy a printed book, Kindle version, or the audio version. Memberships can be purchased that allow 24 audible books to be downloaded per year for less than $250 a year. Credits will roll over each year but be sure to review the conditions on Amazon's website. Purchasing used books is also a more economical method to buy new books or books that are out of print. Amazon has numerous agreements with used-book dealers, so finding that perfect book should be simple.

A typical entry into the full-time solo consulting field can take 3–6 months before business really takes off and over a year until your prior salary is replaced. Patience and enough money to get you by in the short term will pay off in the long run. The initial work, as you start your business, will be getting your business setup and running. Most small companies today are a limited-liability company and can be set up through an attorney and an accountant. They can help you with getting the tax identification number you will need to file your taxes and to give to customers so they can pay you. While you are working on getting the company setup you can work on your website, design your business cards, and develop brochures and flyers to market the company. Remember as a solo consultant all of this will fall under your responsibility. If you work for a consulting company, they will take care of the marketing, website, and attracting the business.

Another important tool for a consultant is a laptop. It must be lightweight and have enough battery power to last all day. Dell makes an excellent laptop for those needing the Windows operating system. I have used a Dell XPS13 for years that would last all day long and would boot up quickly. It was lightweight and had a backlit keyboard. It can also drive a 4K display that will basically mimic four different displays. You will have to purchase Microsoft Office to have the Word, Excel, and PowerPoint applications. For those needing a Macintosh, Apple has several models to fit your needs. I have used a MacBook Air for several years and it also has long battery life, has backlit keyboard, is lightweight, and has the ability to drive a 4K display. As a bonus, Apple puts their equivalent office suite at no charge with the laptop. If you still need Microsoft Office, Microsoft sells a version for the Mac. Each of these laptops retail for just under $1000.

Your office will also need to have a printer and scanner. Many printer companies have a multifunction unit that can print, scan, and fax. Buying a model that allows you to scan documents through an automatic feeder is a big advantage. It will save you the time of scanning each sheet individually. Typically these multifunction printers can save a scanned document in PDF or JPG format. Most of these multifunction printers can be bought for less than $200 each.

As a consultant, many hospitals and companies will require you to have insurance. You should obtain a quote for professional liability insurance from your insurance provider. This will usually run from $500 to $1000 a year.

Another important part of being an independent consultant is marketing materials. This would include your business cards, brochures, and flyers.
You will have to design that material but then you can outsource the printing to a local print shop or search on the Internet for companies to help you
develop and print them. Part of marketing your business cards, brochures,
and flyers will be the use of your company logo. Many companies, local and
on the Internet, can help with the design of a logo suitable for your company. I have used several companies on the Internet and had logos designed
for less than $300.

Once you get your business setup then you will have to rely on the contacts you have developed from networking to solicit business. You will also
have to cold-call hospitals to solicit business, especially when you first start
out in consulting. You will need to do some research to find out where the
HTM department reports to at the hospital. This is who you would contact
for business. They will have the budget and decision authority on the hiring
of consultants. This could be the chief nursing officer, the chief operating
officer, the director of engineering, and sometimes the chief information
officer. Occasionally the director or manager of HTM will need a consultant to help with their operations, but typically it will be someone higher
up in the organization.

The hardest job will always be getting the first contract. Once you have
started building up enough business, then you will see that much of your
business will be through referrals from prior customers. Many solo consultants spend a significant amount of time soliciting for business. Most are
probably only spending 25%–50% of their time actually doing consulting
work. The balance of their time is spent soliciting for new business, working
on their website, writing articles, publishing books, speaking at conferences,
and continuing their education.

As a consultant, your services can include offering advice on medical
equipment replacement strategies, preventive maintenance strategies, policy and procedure development, selection of a computerized maintenance
management system (CMMS), personnel staffing, benchmarking operations,
leadership development and coaching, financial review of HTM operations,
and compliance with The Joint Commission (2018), Det Norske Veritas
(DNV, 2018), Centers for Medicare & Medicaid Services (CMS, 2018),
AABB (2018), or other regulatory agencies.

An example of this could be when a hospital consults with you to determine if the expense for medical equipment is too high. You would review
the budget, staffing, salaries, contracts, parts spent, and training to determine

where the money is being spent. You might determine that the hospital has too many contracts and recommend the reduction of those contracts by insourcing the work to existing staff, by hiring additional staff, or by changing the contract from the original equipment manufacturer to a third-party vendor who could provide similar work at a discounted price. You would need to develop a pro forma (Investopedia, 2018) that outlines the cost of the plan (additional staff, training, and any cost to cancel contracts) and compare this with the savings obtained by changing their current operations. You would typically describe the first-year savings (savings minus start-up costs) and then in subsequent annual savings.

Helping hospitals with medical equipment replacement strategies is another task that can be performed. Typically hospitals have more capital equipment that needs to be replaced than dollars allocated to the capital budget. Your expertise in this area can help the hospital decide the best strategy on when and what to purchase. You could also offer advice on extending the life of their medical equipment through the use of third-party parts and/or third-party service. You would work closely with the HTM department and the c-suite in evaluating and recommending a solution to their medical equipment replacement. This would include short-term and long-term strategies.

Cybersecurity is a very big concern for hospitals today (Busdicker and Upendra, 2017). As a consultant, you would work with the HTM department and the information technology (IT) department to develop physical and software solutions to minimize the risk of patient information being stolen. You would work with the team to physically inventory the medical equipment that operates on a network and capture all vital data needed by the IT department. This would include media access control (MAC) addresses, Internet Protocol (IP) addresses, operating system version and patch levels, antivirus information, and what type of physical security is used for the device. This can be done by manually entering the data into the database or through software that resides on the network and obtains the equipment information automatically (Swim, 2012).

Best practice is another method that you can consult with hospitals. AAMI offers a guide to determine the level at which an HTM department operates called the HTM Levels Guide. It was developed with the help of clinical engineers, consultants, AAMI staff, AAMI Technology Management Council, and others to help identify and guide the department through the three levels: fundamental, established and advanced. The most advanced HTM programs manage all medical equipment costs from their budget regardless of the level of service. This would include typical medical equipment, anesthesia equipment, imaging equipment, laboratory equipment, endoscopes, and sterilizers. The guide is available for download free from the AAMI website (AAMI, 2018).

Benchmarking an HTM department is extremely important to a hospital. Questions to ask include the following:

- Are they operating efficiently compared with other similar-sized organizations?
- Are they staffed with the proper mix of management and technical staff?
- Is the HTM department routinely analyzing their customer satisfaction and developing a plan to improve their services to the clinical departments and the c-suite?
- Are the nursing and clinical departments happy with the turnaround time on the repair of their medical equipment?
- How does the employee retention compare?
- Are their employees happy with the pay and recognition?
- What type of reward and recognition has been developed and used in the department?
- Is the HTM department routinely rounding on the departments?

Your job would be to analyze, report, and recommend best practices in all these areas. You can keep up to date on the current best practices by reading several of the trade magazines on medical equipment management by subscribing to AAMI's Biomedical Instrumentation & Technology, Tech Nation, and 24 × 7 Magazine. Also attending the conferences held by AAMI (AAMI's annual conference is held once a year) and Tech Nation (MD Expo is held twice a year) will keep you current on the best practices.

Ensuring the hospital is compliant with regulatory standards is another strategy you can use to help hospitals and clinics. You must be up to date on the latest guidance, standards, and regulations to ensure compliance and be able to suggest ways for hospitals to become in compliance. You can download the latest medical equipment standards from The Joint Commission for a fee. This would need to be performed annually. You must be able to read and write a medical equipment management plan (MEMP) that will show compliance. You will then need to audit the program for compliance and the reporting of routine reports and an end-of-year overview. The Joint Commission (2018) has several audit tools you can purchase on their website. AAMI has several examples of an MEMP that you can download. You can find them under Membership & Community then HTM Resources.

You will find information on communication, equipment inspections, marketing your department, policies, promoting safety, and service agreements.

CMS, DNV, and The Joint Commission routinely update the requirements of medical equipment in the hospital. One recent change was the use of an Alternative Equipment Maintenance (AEM) strategy. You should be able to develop and analyze an AEM that may or may not be in place at the hospital to ensure compliance. AAMI provides an overview of how to develop a successful AEM program for an HTM department (AAMI, 2018). Power strips or relocatable power taps (RPTs) are another recent requirement of CMS to manage. The November 2017 issue of AAMI News had an article on how to develop a policy and manage RPTs. Understanding the requirements and the responsibilities of the hospital is key to successfully pass an inspection.

Alarm fatigue is a big concern for clinical staff at hospitals. Studies show 85%–95% of alarms is little more than wild goose chases (Venella, 2017). The constant alarming of patient monitoring and other medical equipment can easily overwhelm the clinical staff. You would work with clinical staff, the HTM department, risk management, human factors staff, and regulatory compliance staff to develop and analyze an effective program to ensure that the alarms are properly managed and set for the safe use of their medical equipment.

Here are some recommendations to address this issue:
- Form an alarm committee at your hospital consisting of HTM, nursing, risk management, and a human factors expert.
- Collect baselines of alarm settings for all medical equipment.
- Collect all policies on alarm management.
- Collect alarm data from log files on medical equipment through the HTM department or medical equipment vendor.
- Provide the alarm data to the team and share with any necessary nursing or respiratory therapy councils.
- Analyze the data.
- Provide recommendations to the committee based on the findings.
- Update policies and procedures around alarm management including who has the responsibility to change alarm settings.
- Finally, do not forget to educate the clinical staff on the new changes to the policies around alarm management.

Leadership coaching is another avenue to help out an HTM department. Usually a biomedical equipment technician or clinical engineer is promoted to a manager or director position over an HTM department but will not always have the leadership and management skills needed to effectively manage an HTM department. Your job would be to coach and teach the new manager on the skills needed for this new position. This would include the understanding of the MEMP, reporting and developing metrics for regulatory compliance to the Environment of Care Committee, managing employees, understating return on investment, and writing policies and procedures. AAMI offers a Certified Healthcare Technology Manager study guide for new managers to become certified. It was written by Pat Lynch and is available on AAMI website. AAMI also offers a free download of all the requirements for any certification [Certified Biomedical Equipment Technician (CBET), Certified Radiology Equipment Specialist (CRES), Certified Laboratory Equipment Specialist (CLES), and Certified Healthcare Technology Manager (CHTM)] on its website, which gives the outline of each test and reference materials. Both these sources offer a great outline of what is required for an HTM manager.

The database used by the HTM department, typically called CMMS, is one of the most important tools used by HTM. It will include the inventory of medical equipment, equipment history, the reporting capability, scheduling of preventive maintenance, end of support information, IT information such as IP and MAC address, purchase information including cost and initial date of inventory, and the physical location of the device (Lipschultz, 2014). The CMMS is used to comply with recalls of medical equipment and to ensure compliance with CMS, DNV, and The Joint Commission requirements. A consultant's role would be to evaluate the current CMMS used by the HTM department and ensure that it meets the needs of the organization (Cohen, 2014). Several CMMS vendors now offer integration with medical equipment test equipment to automate the data captured during preventive maintenance testing. Some also integrate with medical equipment on the IT network to capture information from connected devices (Malhotra, 2018). AAMI offers webinars and handbooks to help with the selection and requirements of a good CMMS.

A consultant can work for a company that offers its services to healthcare systems or you can work as a one-person company. The advantage of working for a company is you would have more resources at your disposal and you have a benefits package. The advantage of working for yourself is you can determine your salary, your schedule, and the type of work you do. The downside is you will need to not only provide and pay for your own benefits but also provide for the marketing and selling of your business.

Many consultants work out of an office setup in their home. This will save the expense of renting an office space. This saves a lot of time on commuting to and from an office, but it should be a dedicated office and not a room shared by the family. A typical consultant will travel much of the time but some of the work can be performed at home or via a web camera.

A consultant needs to have a presence on the Internet so a website is essential. The website can be setup by yourself or you can outsource the operation to a website developer. The website should include who you are, what professional services you provide, an overview of experiences, and how to contact you. Developing a website is not that difficult and a simple online search will offer many companies that will allow you to build it yourself or outsource the operation to them.

EXPERT WITNESS

Another option for an HTM professional is to work as an expert witness. An expert witness is defined as someone who is qualified as an expert by knowledge, skill, experience, training, or education and may testify in the form of an opinion or otherwise if (1) the expert's scientific, technical, or other specialized knowledge will help the trier of fact to understand the evidence or to determine a fact in issue; (2) the testimony is based on sufficient facts or data; (3) the testimony is the product of reliable principles and methods; and (4) the expert has reliably applied the principles and methods to the facts of the case (Federal Evidence, 2018).

Becoming an expert witness will require a broad knowledge and experience of medical equipment, the regulations governing medical equipment, the proper operation of medical equipment, and a solid understanding of engineering. Typically the expert witness will have many years of experience in the operation and management of medical equipment. This work can be done as a part-time or full-time job. Many expert witnesses in healthcare technology are also registered as a professional engineer.

Assuming you meet the criteria of knowledge and expertise, the next step to start out as an expert witness is becoming known. You need to develop a website that should give a good overview of your qualifications and expertise you can bring to clients. You will still have to market your services, so joining a professional listing of expert witnesses will greatly help you become known.

An expert witness is usually used during a lawsuit between a medical equipment manufacturer and a hospital or client when a piece of medical equipment is suspected in causing harm to a patient. An expert witness is able to investigate each of the product life stages starting with design considerations and manufacturing quality control, and continuing with postmarket complaints management and the fulfillment of the owner's responsibilities. The expert witness will then provide an explanation of the causes in a language in which both judge and jury can understand (BioMedEng, 2018).

Many court cases will not require an expert witness. An article in Biomedical Instrumentation & Technology from 2006 states that probably less than 10% of lawsuits will ever require the disposition of a witness. If you are called to testify just remember these recommendations:

- Review the adherence to standards, policies, and procedures.
- Review training of clinical staff and support staff.
- Review records of documentation of service.
- Review any reports compiled on the incident.
- Report the facts in an easy-to-understand language for the judge, attorneys, and jury (Vockley, 2006).

As an expert witness, you could work for either the plaintiff or the defendant, providing expert testimony in a case about medical equipment, its proper use, and the use of accessories. As an expert witness, be sure to prepare defending your findings against the defense attorney, as the defense attorney will try to disprove your competence. Your attorney should prepare you for this.

An excellent source for more information on medical equipment accidents was published in 2002 by the esteemed Leslie Geddes, DSc. The book is out of print but copies can be found on the Internet by searching by his name or for the title of the book *Medical Device Accidents and Illustrative Cases*.

MEDCIAL EQUIPMENT PLANNER

Medical equipment planners are another option for an HTM professional to pursue. Medical equipment planners work with architects, hospital executives, nursing and clinical staff, vendors, and engineers to select medical equipment for a new hospital or for the expansion of an existing hospital or clinic. The medical equipment planner can work for a large company that offers these services or may decide to do it alone and form a one-person company. Medical equipment planners work all over the world so the ability to travel and stay away from home is important.

When a hospital or clinic is being designed or renovated a medical equipment planner is brought in early to help develop a rough budget on medical equipment. As the design is progressing, specific equipment is recommended based on input from physicians, nurses, clinical staff, and many times HTM staff.

The equipment planner would also work with architects on the design of the hospital or clinic and where the medical equipment will be installed, IT used to support the medical equipment, network closets to house network switches, and the design of nursing stations. The equipment planner would ensure that enough power, medical gases, water, ventilation, and adequate steam pressure are planned for the specific equipment being utilized in the plan.

Developing and designing of low-voltage closets is very important in the support of patient monitoring and nurse call systems. Low-voltage closets are typically the same as a traditional IT closet but are specifically used in medical equipment infrastructure and nurse call systems. Many times, they are located next to a traditional IT closet that houses the switches and routers used for the hospital network. This helps minimize cable runs from the IT network to the medical equipment and nurse call equipment networks. Being able to work with an architect early in the project will allow the proper design of these closets. Best practice would be to have closets above each other on each floor to minimize cable length. You must understand basic networking principles such as the maximum cable length of copper network runs to design the correct network closets. As the maximum length of a copper network cable is 100 m, you must ensure no cables exceed that length when designing or reviewing the network drawings. Understanding the need for emergency power and the heating and cooling requirements of these closets is also critical. Physical security of these closets is also important. Who needs to have access to these closets? It should only be the HTM department or vendors with their equipment in those closets.

A typical nursing station design might have a computer for patient monitoring to track a patient's vital signs; a nurse call system to allow the patient to call the nurse or contact the nurse when the patient gets out of bed; cameras to monitor remote rooms or for security; a real-time location system used to track equipment, staff, and patients; and computers to input nursing records. You would work with the clinical staff and architects to locate where the staff would like the computers and monitoring equipment. You would then work with the architects to designate network drops, power requirements, and any location for the mounting or storage of the computer equipment.

Sometimes the equipment planner also designs a central monitoring area (sometimes called a war room or mission control room) that is a centralized location to track all the patients in the hospital who are on telemetry or other vital signs monitoring. This frees the nurses on the floor from having a dedicated monitoring tech on each floor and is a productive and economical way to monitor patients. Designing a central station monitoring room will involve working with the nurses, architect, and IT staff and facilities engineering. You will need to understand the workflow of the monitoring technicians and should allow ample room for keyboards, mouses, desktop computers, telephones, and multiple displays mounted on a wall. Ample power that is on emergency power and backed up with an uninterruptible power supply is vital to ensure 24×7 operation. Ergonomics are also very important because staff will be sitting in a chair watching the central monitors for at least 8 h a day.

An integrated operating room is another example of the work a medical equipment planner may perform. They will work with physicians, clinical staff, specialists, medical equipment vendors, engineers, and HTM staff to combine higher end imaging equipment (CT and MRI) with existing medical equipment to merge the images onto larger displays in the operating room. This can be very complex because of the different video interfaces used by the different manufacturers of those devices. Typically a video integration device is used to display the images on large LCD screens in the room. All of this must be performed while minimizing cables that could be damaged from movement and equipment bumping into the operating room overhead lights.

REHABILITATION ENGINEER

Rehabilitation is another avenue an HTM professional can take in their career. Rehabilitation engineers help to develop solutions to those with disabilities. According to the Rehabilitation Engineering and Assistive Technology Society of North America (RESNA), rehabilitation engineering is the systematic application of engineering sciences to design, develop, adapt, test, evaluate, apply, and distribute technological solutions to problems confronted by individuals with disabilities in functional areas, such as mobility, communications, hearing, vision, and cognition, and in activities associated with employment, independent living, education, and integration into the community (RESNA, 2018).

This could involve the design or installation of an environmental control unit (ECU) device for persons with a disability to control their environment. This could include operating a telephone, using a computer, turning on and off lights, or adjusting the heating and cooling in a home. The ECU provides independence to persons with a disability rather than relying on family or caregivers to do these functions for them. The ECU can be controlled by voice command, selecting a menu option via an input device, or via a remote control.

Several devices are on the market today that allow this type of home automation using smart devices (Wikipedia, 2018). Amazon offers several devices (Amazon, 2018) that can control smart devices either directly or indirectly with a smart hub. Google (2018), Apple (2018), and other companies are also introducing similar devices. Wink (2018), Samsung (2018), Philips (Meet Hue, 2018), and several other major companies offer smart hubs that operate on the Z-Wave (2018) or Zigbee (2018) protocol with smart devices that can turn on and off lights, operate smart thermostats, detect water leaks, lock and unlock doors, and operate garage doors. A smart hub is a device that operates via a traditional network (wired or wireless) and then transmits the correct protocol (Z-Wave or Zigbee) to a smart device.

For example, you could use an Amazon Echo connected to your wireless network communicating with a Wink smart hub. You would replace your traditional light bulbs with a smart light bulb (Wink, 2018). After configuration, you would tell the Amazon Echo device, "Alexa, turn on sofa lamp," and the sofa lamp would come on. You also have the ability to configure the lights to come on and off at certain times (such as on at dusk and off at dawn) and the ability to brighten or dim the light with a voice command. For lights that are operated by a wired light switch, several companies offer solutions to replace the traditional light switch with a smart light switch that can be controlled by a smart hub. If you have four can lights in your living room, you could replace the light switch with a smart light switch and then control the operation of the canned lights via your voice through your Amazon, Google, Apple, or other smart device. It could be as simple as, "Alexa, turn on living room lights."

For those with speech disabilities, there are more elaborate ECUs that offer a variety of input methods such as a sip and puff switch, soft-touch switches that can be operated by the hand, and even switches that can be operated by the head. A Sip-and-Puff or Sip "n" Puff is assistive technology used to send signals to a device using air pressure by "sipping" (inhaling) or "puffing" (exhaling) on a straw, tube, or "wand." It is primarily used by people who do not have the use of their hands. It is commonly used to control a motorized wheelchair by quadriplegics with very high injury to their spinal cord or people with amyotrophic lateral sclerosis (Wikipedia, 2018). Sip and puff switches are commonly used in hospitals so that a disabled patient can contact the nurse or caregiver through the nurse call system.

Usually a rehabilitation engineer will work with an occupational therapist and physical therapists to help design a treatment solution for persons with a disability. The rehabilitation engineer also works closely with insurance companies and government agencies to help pay for the design and installation of these devices. This work could involve working with the therapists and patients at a rehabilitation hospital or even at their home.

A rehabilitation engineer can also design mobility and seating solutions for persons with a disability. Motorized wheelchairs offer persons with a disability the independence to move about the house or around the neighborhood. The motorized wheelchair can be operated by a sip and puff switch or by a joystick. Seating for wheelchairs is also important so they can prevent pressure ulcers and provide the proper posture corrections needed. This is typically done through a prescription by a physician and then with the guidance of an occupational therapist or physical therapists and a rehabilitation engineer (Wheelchair, 2018). Computer-aided design can be used to help design the proper seating for persons with a disability through the evaluation of pressure points and posture. Their assessment will provide the best solutions for the patient through the analysis of seating pressure distribution, support, and posture. These services are usually paid for by Medicare or through private insurance.

Computer access is another important tool for those with disabilities. A rehabilitation engineer would work with an occupational therapist and the client in developing the right solution. This could involve specialized input devices such as adaptive keyboards, specialized mouses, voice operation, eye movement, or special switches that allow the person to operate a computer. This could also involve modifying the environment around the workstation to allow easier access to a computer.

Another device a rehabilitation engineer can specify and install is a lift device. A lift can assist the caregiver in safely getting a disabled patient in and out of a bed, in and out of a shower or bathtub, and on and off a toilet. A lift device can be ceiling mounted, wall mounted, or a portable device to be used throughout the home. They can be used independently or with the help of a caregiver.

It would also be a good idea to join RESNA to stay current on rehabilitation engineering. RESNA offers continuing education through conferences and even certification as an Assistive Technology Professional (ATP) (RESNA, 2018). The ATP exam covers the following areas of knowledge requirements (RESNA, 2018).

"Assistive technology" includes but is not limited to
- augmentative and alternative communication
- accessible transportation (public and private)
- aids to daily living/activities of daily living
- cognitive aids
- computer access
- electronic aids to daily living
- environmental aids
- learning and study aids
- recreation and leisure
- seating, positioning, and mobility
- sensory (e.g., hearing, vision, physical) aids and accommodations
- vocational aids and accommodations

Ongoing support will be required to support all these devices. This would include initial training and setup of the devices, technical support after the sale, and any modification of the devices after use. Usually the rehabilitation engineer is an authorized representative of specialized manufacturers of devices for persons with a disability and will operate as the consultant, installer, and support of their devices.

FORENSIC ENGINEERING

Forensic engineering is another route to take as an HTM professional. Forensic engineering is defined as the investigation of materials, products, structures, or components that fail or do not operate or function as intended, causing personal injury or damage to property (Wikipedia, 2018). An HTM professional specializing in forensic engineering could work for a company or be an independent consultant.

One example of this would be to investigate a burn on a patient during a surgery involving an electrosurgical unit (ESU) (Wikipedia, 2018). An ESU uses current created by an ESU flowing from an electrosurgical dispersive pencil through the patient and back via an electrosurgical dispersive pad connected to the ESU. For the device to work as intended the electrosurgical dispersive pad is usually placed on a large muscular region, such as a thigh; the proper pencil is inserted into the ESU; and the proper tip is firmly seated into the pencil. The patient should also be isolated from ground so the current only flows from the ESU to the patient and back to the ESU. Any source of external grounding could cause the device not to work properly or could cause a burn to the patient or operator. Another common cause of burns is at the pad site. If the pad is not firmly seated onto the patient the high impedance could cause a burn or make the ESU to not properly operate. The high impedance could be caused by an unshaven area where the dispersive pad would be placed or by the dispersive pad becoming unseated from the body. Most new model ESUs have an impedance circuit built into the ESU to determine and alert the operator if it is working correctly.

An HTM professional could be called in to investigate the cause of the accident and to identify ways to prevent it in the future. The HTM professional would rely on investigation of the ESU operator's techniques and training, review any reports from the hospital or clinic risk manager, review the ESU manufacturer's operator's manual, review the preventive maintenance and service history of the ESU, look at all the supplies used during the surgery, and possibly review any known incidents involving ESU and supplies by searching the Manufacturer and User Facility Device Experience (MAUDE) database from the United States Food and Drug Administration (Access Data, 2018).

The HTM professional would then document his or her findings and give them to the hospital, vendors, risk management, and/or legal representatives.

JOB BOARDS AND SOCIAL MEDIA

Social media is a great source to get business contacts and to keep abreast of changes in your industry. LinkedIn is probably the most preferred social media or "business social media" used by business professionals. If used correctly, you can follow areas of your interest. It is a great way to stay on top of the current issues from AAMI, ACCE, ASHE, ACHE, HIMMS, IMC, and others.

Interests

Operations Consulting Worldwide
7,266 members

Clinical Engineering Management
3,445 members

American Society for Healthcare E...
2,185 followers

Future BMETs Texas State Technica...
69 members

Healthcare Technology Manageme...
36 members

Medical Imaging & Medical Device
5,094 members

See all

But do not forget about Facebook. You can create a business Facebook account to supplement your business website. Along with this, you can add a Twitter account and blog about your business. Many successful freelancers and large businesses are all using these social media outlets to reach more customers.

A book named Social BOOM! by Jeffrey Gitomer is a great resource to get numerous ideas on how to use social media to boost yourself and your company.

Here are a few other sources to help with getting your name out there.

HelpAReporter (https://www.helpareporter.com/)

Signing up is free and reporters can contact you for information. You can sign up for different interests and get three emails a day to answer questions.

FlexJobs (https://www.flexjobs.com/)

You can choose monthly, quarterly, or annual billing. Prices range from $14.95 a month to $49.95 annually. After setting up your profile, you can then monitor your dashboard for the type of job you would like. Jobs range from freelancing, temporary, work from home, and others that just need flexible work schedules. FlexJobs also offers tips, resources, articles, and tools to help find that perfect job. They also offer discounts with many major vendors such as Dell, CostCo, QuickBooks, and WeWork.

Here are some top sites for companies to find freelancers:

UpWork (https://www.upwork.com/)

LocalSolo (https://localsolo.com)

Expert360 (https://expert360.com/), used for companies looking for freelancers and for freelancers seeking jobs

TalMix (https://www.talmix.com/), for companies seeking freelancers

All these companies offer different pricing strategies for how you find companies and what commission you pay back to them.

Finally do not forget about Indeed.com. Although this site is specifically for people looking for full-time jobs, you can also search it for consulting opportunities.

COMPENSATION

According to a study performed by Glassdoor in 2012, an HTM consultant would average $76,292 per year plus additional compensation averaging $5848. This study was based on 479 salaries submitted to Glassdoor (2012). The lowest salary was $49,000 a year and the highest was $120,000 a year.

Your compensation will depend on several factors, such as your experience, the number of jobs you complete, and the rate you are charging your clients.

There are several methods to increase your compensation instead of just completing a work assignment. These could include
- developing and charging for a newsletter
- selling studies to clients
- speaking
- publishing books

The pay scale for an expert witness in the medical field averages $555 an hour compared with an average of $248 for nonmedical experts (SEAK).

The pay scale for a medical equipment planner averaged $61,993 according to less than 20 profiles at Paysa.com. At the 25th percentile, it was $52,476 and at the 75th percentile, it was $69,978; the top earners were at $79,655. About 7% of the medical equipment planners held only a high-school diploma, 33% held a bachelor's degree, 47% held a master's degree, and 7% held a master of business administration (MBA) degree (Paysa).

The pay scale for a rehabilitation engineer averaged $81,505 according to less than 20 profiles at Paysa.com. At the 25th percentile it was $70,150 and at the 75th percentile, it was $91,186; the top earners were at $102,609. About 80% of the rehabilitation engineers held bachelor's degrees, whereas 20% held master's degrees (Payas).

The pay scale for a forensic engineer averages to $82,768 according to Glassdoor.com. According to 446 salaries submitted anonymously to Glassdoor, the lowest was $62,000 and the highest was $110,000 (Glassdoor, 2018).

CONCLUSION

Freelancing as an HTM consultant can be a very rewarding career during or after working at a hospital, medical equipment manufacturer, or third-party HTM company. The ability to set your schedule and decide on what projects you take on can be a great career choice. Many successful HTM professionals have transitioned as an HTM consultant and are making a big impact on the care of medical equipment.

References

AABB, 2018. http://www.aabb.org/Pages/default.aspx.
AAMI, 2018. http://my.aami.org/store/detail.aspx?id=AEM.
AAMI, 2018. http://www.aami.org/.
AAMI, 2018. http://www.aami.org/productspublications/content.aspx?ItemNumber=388
    7&token=fcv$P$7l/u4AErU1J1wBuzf10v9dSLbTIJ.
ACCE, 2018. http://accenet.org.
Access Data, 2018. https://www.accessdata.fda.gov/scripts/cdrh/cfdocs/cfmaude/search.cfm.
ACHE, 2018. http://www.ache.org/.
Amazon, 2018. https://www.amazon.com/Amazon-Echo-And-Alexa-Devices/b?ie=UTF
    8&node=9818047011.

Apple, 2018. https://www.apple.com/homepod/.

ASHE, 2018. http://www.ashe.org/.

BioMedEng, 2018. http://www.biomedeng.com/litigation_support.php.

Busdicker, M., Upendra, P., 2017. The role of healthcare technology management in facilitating medical device cybersecurity. Biomedical Instrumentation and Technology: CyberVigilance: Keeping Healthcare Technology Safe and Secure in a Connected World 51 (s6), 19–25.

CMS, 2018. https://www.cms.gov/.

Cohen, T., March/April 2014. The basics of CMMS. Biomedical Instrumentation and Technology 48 (2), 117–121.

Dickey, D.M., Jagiela, S., Fetters, D., September 2003. Biomedical Instrumentation and Technology 37 (5), 329–337.

DNV GL Healthcare, 2018. http://www.dnvglhealthcare.com/.

Dyro, J.F., 2004. Clinical Engineering Handbook. Elsevier Academic Press, p. 42.

Federal Evidence, 2018. http://federalevidence.com/rules-of-evidence#Rule702.

Glassdoor, 2012. https://www.glassdoor.com/Salaries/healthcare-management-consultant-salary-SRCH_KO0,32.htm.

Glassdoor, 2018. https://www.glassdoor.com/Salaries/forensic-engineer-salary-SRCH_KO0,17.htm.

Google, 2018. https://store.google.com/us/category/home_entertainment?hl=en-US.

HIMSS, 2018. http://www.himss.org/.

IMC USA, 2018. http://www.imcusa.org/.

Investopedia, 2018. https://www.investopedia.com/terms/p/proforma.asp.

Joint Commission, 2018. https://www.jointcommission.org/.

Joint Commission, 2018. https://www.jointcommission.org/.

Lipschultz, A., September/October 2014. Computerized maintenance management systems—design features for HTM. Biomedical Instrumentation and Technology 48 (5), 384–388.

Malhotra, V., January/February 2018. CTO foresees future of CMMS-enabled 'true interoperability'. Biomedical Instrumentation and Technology 52 (1), 60–62.

Meet Hue, 2018. https://www2.meethue.com/en-us.

Paysa. https://www.paysa.com/salaries/medical-equipment-planner–t.

Payas. https://www.paysa.com/salaries/rehabilitation-engineer–t.

RESNA, 2018. http://www.resna.org/resources-definitions.

RESNA, 2018. http://www.resna.org/atp-general-info.

RESNA, 2018. http://www.resna.org/get-certified/atp/exam-outline/exam-outline.

Samsung, 2018. https://www.samsung.com/us/smart-home/smartthings/.

SEAK. https://www.seak.com/expert-witness-fee-study/.

Swim, R., July/August 2012. Keeping data secure: protected health information and medical equipment. Biomedical Instrumentation and Technology 46 (4), 278–280.

Venella, J., 2017. Drawing up a new game plan to reduce alarm fatigue. Biomedical Instrumentation and Technology: Clinical Alarms: Managing the Overload 51 (s2), 71–72.

Vockley, M., November 2006. Called to Testify? Biomedical Instrumentation and Technology 40 (6), 429–434.

Wheelchair, 2018. https://www.wheelchairnet.org/WCN_ProdServ/Consumers/evaluation.html#anchor9029397.

Wikipedia, 2018. https://en.wikipedia.org/wiki/Electrosurgery.

Wikipedia, 2018. https://en.wikipedia.org/wiki/Forensic_engineering.

Wikipedia, 2018. https://en.wikipedia.org/wiki/Smart_device.

Wikipedia, 2018. https://en.wikipedia.org/wiki/Sip-and-puff.

Wink, 2018. https://www.wink.com/.

Wink, 2018. https://www.wink.com/products/.

Zigbee, 2018. http://www.zigbee.org/.

Z-Wave, 2018. http://www.z-wave.com/.

RESOURCES AND LINKS

This chapter provides resources and links for those seeking a career in biomedical engineering.

A LIST OF RELEVANT WEBSITES TO CHECK OUT

Careers in Cybersecurity: https://www.nist.gov/itl/applied-cyber security/nice.

US Biomedical Engineering Society (BMES): https://www.bmes.org/.

FDA website for medical devices:https://www.fda.gov/MedicalDevices/default.htm.

The Best Undergraduate Biomedical Engineering Programs. US News and World Report Rankings: https://www.usnews.com/best-colleges/rankings/engineering-doctorate-biological-biomedical.

List of accredited biomedical engineering schools: Career Index: https://www.educationnews.org/career-index/biomedical-engineering-schools/.

Link for website of interest to those seeking a career: https://www.nist.gov/itl/applied-cybersecurity/nice.

Link to Khana Academy: https://www.khanacademy.org/computing/computer-programming/sql.

Link to Vertabelo Academy: https://academy.vertabelo.com/blog/top-5-sql-jobs-high-salaries/.

Link to maintsmart.com: https://www.maintsmart.com/?gclid=EAIaIQobChMIkZ3wxOnU2wIVjluGCh2YEgwNEAMYASAAEgLM2vD_BwE.

Link to officetrax: https://www.officetrax.com/Maintenance/Overview/CMMS?gclid=EAIaIQobChMIo7nEo-_U2wIVgQOGCh37DAldEAAYAyAAEgLLOPD_BwE.

A LIST OF SOME OF THE ASSOCIATIONS IN THE BIOMEDICAL ENGINEERING FIELD

HIMSS: www.himss.org.
AAMI: www.aami.org.
ACCE: www.acce.org.

A LIST OF SIGNIFICANT REPORTS, STUDIES, AND INFOGRAPHICS

Secure Medical Device Deployment report: https://www.owasp.org/images/c/c3/SecureMedicalDeviceDeployment.pdf.

State of Cybersecurity 2017 infographic: https://www.isaca.org/About-ISACA/Press-room/Documents/State-of-Cybersecurity-ifg_eng_0217.pdf.

Article: Designing a Career in Biomedical Engineering by Elisabeth Pain.

SOME IRRELEVANT INFORMATION REGARDING RESOURCES FOR FREELANCERS

Job Boards and Social Media

Social media is a great source to get business contacts and to keep abreast of changes in your industry. LinkedIn is probably the most preferred social media or "business social media" used by business professionals. If used correctly, you can follow the areas of your interest. It is a great way to stay on top of the current issues from the Association for the Advancement of Medical Instrumentation (AAMI), the American College of Clinical Engineering (ACCE), the American Society for Healthcare Engineering (ASHE), the American College of Healthcare Executives (ACHE), the Healthcare Information and Management Systems Society (HIMMS), the Institute of Management Consultants (IMC), and others.

But do not forget about Facebook. You can create a business Facebook account to supplement your business website. Along with this, you can add a Twitter account and blog about your business. Many successful freelancers and large businesses are all using these social media outlets to reach more customers.

A book named *Social BOOM!* by Jeffrey Gitomer is a great resource to get numerous ideas on how to use social media to boost yourself and your company.

Here are a few other resources to help with getting your name out there. HelpAReporter (https://www.helpareporter.com/)

Signing up is free and reporters can contact you for information. You can sign up for different interests and get three emails a day to answer questions.

FlexJobs (https://www.flexjobs.com/)

You can choose monthly, quarterly, or annual billing. Prices range from $14.95 a month to $49.95 annually. After setting up your profile, you can then monitor your dashboard for the type of job you would like. Jobs range from freelancing, temporary, work from home, and others that just need flexible work schedules. FlexJobs also offers tips, resources, articles, and tools to help find that perfect job. It also offers discounts with many major vendors such as Dell, CostCo, QuickBooks, and WeWork.

Here are some top sites for companies to find freelancers:

UpWork (https://www.upwork.com/)

LocalSolo (https://localsolo.com)

Expert360 (https://expert360.com/), used for companies looking for freelancers and freelancers seeking jobs

TalMix (https://www.talmix.com/), for companies seeking freelancers

All these companies offer different pricing strategies for how you find companies and what commission you pay back to them.

Finally do not forget about Indeed.com. Although this site is specifically for people looking for full-time jobs, you can also search it for consulting opportunities.

APPENDICES

A. http://www.bme.uconn.edu/

B. http://accenet.org/Pages/Default.aspx

C. http://www.aami.org/productspublications/articledetail.aspx?Item Number=1016

D. https://www.flexjobs.com/

E. https://www.owasp.org/images/c/c3/SecureMedicalDeviceDeployment. pdf.

F. https://www.isaca.org/About-ISACA/Press-room/Documents/State-of-Cybersecurity-ifg_eng_0217.pdf

G. https://www.nist.gov/itl/applied-cybersecurity/nice

H. https://www.bmes.org/

I. https://www.fda.gov/MedicalDevices/default.htm

J. https://www.usnews.com/best-colleges/rankings/engineering-doctorate-biological-biomedical

K. https://www.educationnews.org/career-index/biomedical-engineering-schools/

Index

Note: 'Page numbers followed by "f" indicate figures, "t" indicate tables.'